THE CULTURAL REVOLUTION COOKBOOK

COOKBOOK

Simple, healthy recipes from China's countryside

Sasha Gong
and
Scott D. Seligman

Food Photography by Charles Cohan Fischl

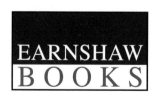

EARNSHAW
BOOKS

THE CULTURAL REVOLUTION COOKBOOK
Copyright © 2011 Sasha Gong and Scott D. Seligman
ISBN-13: 978-988-19984-6-0

First printing December 2011

Published by Earnshaw Books Ltd. (Hong Kong).

Table of Contents

"A Revolution is Not a Dinner Party"
"革命不是请客吃饭"

"Take the classroom into the fields," 1975. "Open the school doors and take the classroom into the fields" was a mid-1970s movement that brought university students and professors into factories and farms to learn firsthand from workers and peasants.

It was Chairman Mao Zedong (1893–1976) who famously wrote this line, and most of those forcibly sent down to the countryside during the Great Proletarian Cultural Revolution of 1966-1976 would surely agree. Most came to feel that leaving their education and professions behind to work side by side with the peasants was a tragic waste of their productive years and an unmitigated disaster for China.

It was, in fact, both of those things. But for many it was not completely devoid of redeeming aspects. Hard toil in the communes was not pleasant, but it was a learning experience for the many city dwellers sent down during that tumultuous decade. And like it or not, it shaped their lives and remains to this day a vital part of their personal histories.

Living among the peasants was difficult, and food was seldom abundant. But those who experienced it learned to make do with what there was. They learned to cook with the fresh, wholesome foods that were in season and to conserve scarce fuel by flash-cooking over a very hot flame. And they learned to prepare remarkably tasty and healthful dishes with enough nourishment to sustain them through long, arduous days in the fields.

The many awful accounts of the bad times, during which people were forced to eat insects and tree bark, were true, but they don't tell the entire story. Living in the countryside made many into frugal cooks who learned to get the best flavors out of low-calorie foods, devoid of chemical preservatives, fresh from the fields and ponds.

These are their recipes. They don't require exotic ingredients; everything you need can be found in a reasonably well-stocked grocery store. The step-by-step instructions are easy to follow, and substitutions are suggested where appropriate. The Cultural Revolution was, indeed, no dinner party, but that didn't stop many Chinese cooks from working culinary wonders with what they did have readily available: the fresh, local, healthy foods of the countryside.

A Personal Story
By Sasha Gong

Guangzhou, 1962: I Learn to Cook

I started my cooking career at age six. The year was 1962, and I had just entered elementary school. My parents, both faculty members at a college in Guangzhou (Canton), had to work from seven in the morning until 11 at night, so nobody was home to take me to school, and nobody was there

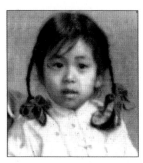

Me at age five. We were living in Guangzhou.

when I got home. My mother gave me instructions on how to whip up breakfast and dinner for myself on our small, coal-burning stove. Breakfast was normally a bowl of noodles with a sprinkling of salt and soy sauce, and a typical dinner might be a bowl of rice with boiled vegetables or an occasional egg. With just a few drops of cooking oil, a fried egg tasted heavenly if one was lucky enough to get one's hands on one. Just a single egg could make my day.

China was just coming out of its worst famine ever, a disastrous consequence of the Great Leap Forward, an exercise in accelerated central planning gone amok that created shortages of nearly everything people needed to live. If coal was hard to get, meat was even harder. One of my brothers, aged five at the time, was questioned in kindergarten about his view of communism, which had of course been held up to all of us as an ideal society. His answer? "Communism is when we all have meat to eat at every meal!" Most of the time, of course, it meant precisely

the opposite. To supplement our meager rations of meat, in fact, I was assigned the duty of feeding four rabbits being raised on our balcony. I gave them fresh grass harvested from the school yard, and when they reached maturity, they were a welcome addition to the family dinner table.

Rabbits weren't the only food people raised at home. During those lean years, most food was rationed, and urbanites like us grew whatever we could in our tiny apartments, on our balconies or – if we were lucky – on small plots of land. People raised chickens, guinea pigs and ducks in their homes and grew chives, squash, eggplant, cucumbers and cabbage. Only grain was off-limits; the government insisted on a monopoly on rice, wheat and other grains, for which you had to line up at city markets and wait for hours before you could get your monthly allotment in exchange for cash and a ration coupon.

Xinqiaohe, Hunan Province, 1965: We are Sent to the Countryside

In 1965, my siblings and I were sent to live with my grandparents because my parents found it too onerous to care for us. Unfortunately, just two months later, my grandfather, a World War II hero who had fought the Japanese in the 1940s, got into political trouble. He was accused by the government – falsely – of being a "counter-revolutionary," and as a consequence lost not only his job, but his right to live in the city, which even today is considered a privilege in China. He was forced to return to the small village in Hunan Province where he had been born, and which he had left in

2

the 1920s. As members of his household, my grandmother, my brothers and sister and I had to go along with him.

Our entire family – six in all – was assigned to a 200-sq. ft. room in a three-room house in the village of Xinqiaohe. Our room came complete with a small pit in which a few chickens slept. Half the kitchen, which we shared with another family, was taken up by a large stove with two burners. There was a huge wok and a smaller pot that kept water warm for bathing and drinking. This was fed from a large water tank (which we children filled every day, bucket by bucket, from a local pond). There was also a wooden table with a slice of a tree trunk we used as a cutting board and a few miscellaneous utensils – a spatula, a ladle and a large pair of chopsticks.

The village had neither a store nor a market, and the closest grocery was a three-hour hike away. So except for a very few items such as salt and soy sauce, virtually everything we ate was produced nearby. Eggs came from the hens pecking for morsels under our dinner table, or for bugs outside. We learned that when a young hen's face turned red, it meant she was about to begin egg production. Occasionally, a hen would refuse to come out of the pit. Two weeks later, she would show up with a dozen noisy chicks, proudly strolling through the neighborhood.

With my cousin in Guangzhou. I was 12.

If food was scarce, grandfather might tell the children to go and collect some eels. We would happily jump barefoot into the shallow water of the nearby rice field and try to catch the slippery creatures between our toes. These eels were most delicious when steamed or stir-fried with chili pepper. Nobody had a refrigerator; smoke, salt, soy sauce and chili pepper were our main preservation agents. Grandfather might hang a fish caught by my brothers over the stove, coat it with salt and let the smoke do the rest of the work. When the flesh of the fish was firm and dry, it would be a choice item on our table for weeks to come.

Jin'er, Guangdong, 1969:
Re-Education by the Peasants

The Cultural Revolution, launched in mid-1966, greatly radicalized the already fanatical political atmosphere in China. During this chaotic period, my siblings and I rejoined our parents in the city of Guangzhou, but in 1968, both my parents – and those of many of my friends – were sent to camps for "re-education through labor," something that happened to the majority of the nation's intellectuals. My siblings and I – we were 14, 12, 10 and 6 at the time – had to live by ourselves in the city. We had a very small allowance from the government, which matched exactly the official poverty line. My sister – later an economist – took care of the finances, and I became the family cook.

Food was scare and rationed. Every morning, I went to the market and waited in several lines to buy it. A few times a week, children from several families would put our meager rations together and create a variety of dishes. On one very memorable occasion, nine of us made more than 300 dumplings, dividing the food evenly among ourselves. Cooking was among very few enjoyable activities in those dark days. From time to time, I found satisfaction in making simple dishes, such as *Tofu with Scallions and Sesame Dressing* (*see page 27*).

In 1969, Chairman Mao Zedong ordered high school students to resettle in the countryside, beginning the exodus

that would eventually send 17 million to rural areas. At age 12, I was too young to be covered by this policy, but I was soon sent with about 100 others my age to a village elsewhere in Guangdong called Jin'er to be "re-educated" by the local peasants. And what a re-education it was! From 1969-1971, I learned to work in the rice fields and to plant vegetables. My team was also charged with building a school and cooking for hundreds of people in communal kitchens.

In Guangdong as in Hunan, nearly everything we ate was locally produced. Rice came from the village paddy, vegetables from family plots and meat from the pigs raised on the collective farm. It was actually processed food that was considered exotic and was highly prized. Machine-made noodles, for example, were served only on important occasions such as birthdays. Noodles are a traditional Chinese symbol of longevity, so a bowl of them with one or two eggs was our version of a "birthday cake" (*see Noodles in Chicken Broth, page 145*). Canned food was a luxury only a small number of well-off, urban professionals could afford. One can of the Chinese version of Spam was considered so nutritious that it could fetch two months' worth of meat rations. Apart from its high price, processed food was rare because of the difficulty of transportation. Things like noodles and crackers could be found only in the county seat, a four-hour round trip by bicycle.

For a short time, young people who had been sent down from the urban areas were assigned to eat with the villagers. Before long, however, the peasants protested, because we ate too much – far more than the ration coupons and money we brought in could buy. So the authorities decided to set up a communal kitchen. We rotated in groups of seven for 10-day stints in the kitchen, during which time we did the cooking instead of going to work in the field. So everyone

Faded slogans still adorn this building in Jin'er more than a quarter century after the end of the Cultural Revolution. This one reads, "Rely on ourselves, fight hard and re-make Jin'er."

got a chance to learn how it was done, and few took advantage of the position by filling their bellies at others' expense. We learned to make the most out of a relatively small palette of available ingredients, including cooking oil, soy sauce, salt, scallions, ginger and a few vegetables. I became particularly proficient with a knife, learning how to slice and chop efficiently. But mostly I learned the surprisingly wide variety of dishes and tastes that could be made with just a few, fresh ingredients, and how to get the best flavors out of what we had.

Guangzhou, 1972: Assigned to a Candy Factory

In 1972, I was allowed to return to Guangzhou and was assigned employment. My school had been allotted a certain number of slots at various enterprises in the city, and I was "allocated" to a collectively run candy factory. A job at a state-owned enterprise would have brought more benefits – housing and a better health plan – but because of my so-called "bad family background," I did not rate a plum job.

I became one of several hundred workers who produced hard and soft candy in three shifts, and I was assigned to the candy forming machines. Every 15 minutes, I had to carry a sixty-pound piece of half-melted candy down a 50-ft. hallway and load it into a 1930s-vintage machine to be molded into peanut brittle, rock candy or fruit chews.

The work was actually pretty interesting, and I loved the independence and the fact that I was earning my own income. Plus, there were ancillary benefits. Sugar – a tightly controlled luxury (the ration was 250 grams, or just under 9 oz. per person per month) – was readily available to consume within the factory. Cooking was one of the most frequent subjects of conversation among the co-workers, who mostly had only a few years' worth of education. It was also one of the few relatively "safe" topics for group discussion. I learned all kinds of tricks from them – that adding starch and water when scrambling eggs would improve their texture, that smashing shrimp with the side of a cleaver before cooking it would tenderize it, which vegetables were good for steaming and which were better for stir-flying, *etc*. We often brought our dishes to the workplace to share.

I not only gained the reputation of being a good cook; I also became known as a bookworm. With only three years of formal education, I read all the books I could put my hands on. These included political treatises, but also Chinese translations of Dostoevsky, Tolstoy, Balzac and John Stuart Mill as well as O. Henry, Tennessee Williams, Mark Twain and Arthur Miller. My pursuit of knowledge, unfortunately, put me on the Party security apparatus' radar screen, and after I joined an underground protest group that was pushing for democracy and rule of law, I got arrested. I was imprisoned by the authorities for almost a year from 1977 to 1978, and I spent my 21st birthday in solitary confinement.

I was held on the third floor of a warehouse near my factory in a makeshift cell about eight feet square with a bed, a desk and a chair. I was allowed no letters, no books, no newspapers and no visitors, and was given pen and paper, but only for the purpose of drafting a confession. The goal was to get me to admit that I had done wrong and to denounce my cohorts, neither of which I was about to do. And the tools employed were endless interrogations, on the one hand, and, on the other, "struggle sessions," in which I was forced on a stage in front of a thousand or so people for hours at a time and accused of harboring bourgeois sentiments and reactionary thoughts.

Members of my underground protest group.

Beijing, 1979 and Cambridge, Massachusetts, 1987: Life Takes a Turn for the Better

I was never actually convicted of any crime, because China was emerging from its insanity and what I had done no longer seemed punishable. My exoneration and release from prison more or less coincided with the end

of the Cultural Revolution. Things then began to return to normal.

In 1978, universities reopened after a 12-year hiatus and millions of young people who had had no opportunity for higher education during that time were allowed to sit for the college entrance exam. I won a spot at Peking University, China's top college. So I packed up my kerosene stove and headed north. Eight years and two degrees later, I landed in the U.S. and entered the Ph.D. program at Harvard University.

My apartment became a gathering place for Chinese students studying in local universities, and it's never been clear to me whether it was my personality or my *Braised Pork in Soy Sauce (see page 67)* that made it so popular. In Boston, finding authentic ingredients for Chinese cooking was easy, but there were also opportunities for experimentation. Balsamic vinegar made all sweet-and-sour dishes taste great – arguably better than Chinese vinegar. Using honey instead of sugar added a special flavor to chicken and duck dishes. And ovens and microwaves saved lots of time and worked just as well as steaming in some dishes.

After graduation it was on to California, and in 1998 I came to Washington, D.C., where I have lived ever since. Several years ago I met Scott Seligman – a career "China hand" who has written extensively about China and speaks two dialects of Chinese – and discovered that he is a pretty talented Chinese cook in his own right, having learned the basics in Taiwan. Scott then spent several years in Hong Kong and Beijing, where he honed his skills and picked up

a lot of tips. We have collaborated on several books, articles and websites, but this is our first cookbook.

We've tried not only to present a retrospective of an important era in China's history, but also to offer up some wonderful recipes from the Chinese countryside as well as some practical tips for preparation and cooking. We wish you kaiwei (开胃) – the Chinese equivalent of "bon appetit"!

Testing a Recipe in Scott's Kitchen

The Cultural Revolution Cookbook

The Cultural Revolution:
A Culinary History

For most Chinese who lived through the Cultural Revolution, the very idea of a history of eating during that cheerless decade sounds like an oxymoron. It was an era in which the traditional food culture of China – which, according to an old Chinese saying, is on a par with heaven – went into near-total eclipse. Shortages were the order of the day, and one was lucky to consume as many calories as one burned on any given day. The art of cooking, in the sense of a body of collected wisdom about ingredients, seasonings and preparation methods, was summarily abandoned and was, in fact, criticized as a capitalist remnant. People ate whatever they could get their hands on, and there was almost never enough to go around.

The challenges, to be sure, were daunting. But the Chinese rose to them, as they have risen to so many others in their long, arduous past, and in so doing they demonstrated remarkable resourcefulness and creativity. It would be a huge mistake to assume that mere shortage of ingredients or fuel stopped Chinese cooks from preparing tasty, nourishing meals. Lack of ingredients was an obstacle, but it engendered a creative search for substitutes. Lack of fuel required that cooking be quick and efficient. Improvisation was required, but the results were often surprisingly good: food, even under less than optimal circumstances, could still be nutritious, flavorful and healthy.

The Roots of Shortage

With its large population and lack of sufficient arable land, China has faced the threat of food shortages and even famine throughout its long history. Droughts, typhoons, blights and plagues have always been facts of life for Chinese peasants, but under Communist rule, poorly conceived and executed government policies overtook even these in the sheer magnitude of their impact. Under the tutelage of its then-ally, the Soviet Union, China unwisely embraced central economic planning, and by the mid-1950s the government had monopolized the purchase, distribution and sale of grain, the lifeblood of the Chinese peasantry. Soon other agricultural commodities like vegetable oil were also controlled, and a system of rationing, not only of grain, but also many other agricultural commodities, had to be introduced.

By the mid-1950s, rural Chinese were forced to re-organize into people's communes. This structure was followed, in 1958, by the disastrous Great Leap Forward, which was an ill-conceived effort to accelerate development that involved confiscation of private land and further collectivization. A combination of ill-advised planting methods, false productivity reports and inane policies that forced peasants to sell more to the government than they could spare resulted in three years of famine – possibly the worst in all human history – in which tens of millions perished.

"Long live the general line, long live the Great Leap Forward, long live the people's communes."

The magnitude of the disaster compelled a re-examination of Chairman Mao Zedong's policies, and he was forced to allow moderate Party officials like Liu Shaoqi and Deng Xiaoping to roll them back somewhat. As peasants were permitted private ownership of small parcels of land and farmers' markets were partially restored, the countryside slowly recovered. But Mao had lost prestige and some of his power in the process, and he found the situation intolerable. He had to bide his time, but his vision of building communism was undimmed, and before long he was up to his old tricks again.

Cultural Revolution and Chaos

In 1966, Mao officially launched the Great Proletarian Cultural Revolution. Billed as a top-down, nationwide movement against "capitalist roaders" and revisionists secretly committed to restoring capitalism, it was actually an effort to purge his political rivals within the Party. There was no shortage of collateral victims. They included traditional enemies of the Communists such as former landlords and intellectuals. Eventually, Party leaders were targeted, too. Mao mobilized China's students, and soon rogue bands of young "Red Guards" roamed the country,

proudly sporting buttons emblazoned with Mao's profile, destroying property, persecuting people and dispensing summary "justice" that often included murdering those they labeled enemies of the state.

As those in authority were purged and sent off to labor camps, societal institutions ceased to function. Schools, factories, restaurants and stores closed their doors, and chaos spread through the countryside as well. It did not take long for the supply of food and consumer goods to dry up. As store shelves emptied, rationing intensified, and extended not only to grain, but also to salt, sugar, eggs, cooking oil, bean curd, soy sauce and nearly everything edible.

"Enthusiastically achieve struggle, criticism and reform!"

By 1968, the students Mao had unleashed on society were completely out of control, and he decided it was necessary to mobilize workers to re-assert authority over them. He also ordered the military to take over the functions of the local governments and impose order. By late 1968, he had cooked up a novel policy that would serve not only to quell the unrest in the cities, but also to ease the urban food shortage and solve the massive unemployment problem all at the same time: he ordered the privileged, urban youth "sent down" to the countryside, where they would work in farming villages and mountainous areas and learn from the peasants. Many would remain there for as long as a decade and would, in time, come to consider themselves a lost generation.

"Sent-Down" Youth in the Countryside

More than 17 million young city dwellers were "sent down" to rural areas throughout the country in the "up to the mountains and down to the villages" movement. It was an eye-opening experience for young people, many of whom were dispatched to areas far from their homes in China's borderlands. Some were sent to large, state-owned farms manned by military veterans; others went to small villages to live with peasant families.

For many, it was the first experience living away from home and, like it or not, an opportunity to learn about country living and pick up some life skills. They discovered where the grain they ate came from and all the effort that went into making it fit for consumption. Students accustomed to buying packaged noodles learned how wheat becomes flour, and how flour, in turn, is made into noodles. They learned how rice is threshed. They struggled with wotou, a tasteless variety of corn bread made

"To the villages we go, to the borderlands we go, to the places in the motherland that need us most we go," 1970.

On December 22, 1968, the People's Daily *announced Mao's policy of sending urban youth to the countryside.*

without oil or sugar that sticks in the throat. And they were introduced to wild plants that were not only tasty, but that had medicinal properties and could cure ailments.

The peasants also taught them how to preserve meat and vegetables by salting, smoking and air-drying them so food would be available in winter and early spring. They learned not to waste anything – not even leftover tea leaves, which can be used to cook eggs, or the water in which rice is rinsed, which can offer nourishment to farm animals. And they learned to bundle straw tightly to minimize the amount of air between the stalks and thus maximize the amount of cooking time it could provide. Nothing was wasted: the ash left behind was recycled for use as fertilizer.

Coping with Rationing

It was a decade characterized by scarcity, but exactly what was scarce varied by location and with time. Some commodities were rationed on a per-person basis. In Guangzhou in 1968, for example, adults were given coupons that could be used, together with cash, to purchase 22-32 catties (about 25-35 lbs., or 11-16 kg.) of rice per month, half a catty (a little more than half a pound, or 600 g.) of cooking oil, half a catty of uncooked pork (but only 70%

A 1975 ration coupon from Jilin Province entitling the bearer to purchase 100 grams of grain.

of that amount if it was cooked), four bean curd cakes and half a catty of fish. Distribution of other items was based on households: each got about 10 small eggs and two fowl – a chicken, duck or goose, one at National Day in October and one in the springtime at Chinese New Year. In the north rice was rare, so the coupons were for flour and coarse grain – generally corn or sorghum.

And then there were accommodations for those with special needs. Muslims got special allocations permitting them to buy beef instead of pork; new mothers got coupons for extra eggs. The sick were given vouchers for milk, eggs, red meat and/or chicken, depending on availability, and infants were permitted milk powder.

Military families and high-ranking government officials generally got slightly larger allotments. Coupons could not be bought or sold under penalty of incarceration, though as a practical matter a black market always existed. The market reforms instituted by Deng Xiaoping after Mao's death broke the back of the rationing system, but it did not disappear entirely until the early 1990s.

Capitalist Grain Trumps Socialist Grass

In the mid-1970s, radicals were asserting, "It's better to grow socialist grass than capitalist grain." While no one would have dared contradict them, many would no doubt have privately disagreed. The sent-down youth had not all been unwilling victims. Spoon-fed Marxism-Leninism and Mao Zedong's thought since childhood, many had believed profoundly in socialism and were willing, if not eager, to build it in China. But experiencing it in practice, side by side with peasants constantly fending off starvation, caused a great many to become disenchanted, and to lose their faith in the doctrine.

In the end, when the Cultural Revolution was over and the sent-down youth were permitted to return to the cities, all but a very few did so readily. Most would think of their time in the countryside as a disastrous waste of a decade, but that view told only part of the story. The experience had also been formative, and they came back more mature and self-reliant. They came back with lifelong friendships, with skills they had never dreamed they would acquire and with a hunger for learning and improving their lots in life that would lead many to great achievements. And many came back with the knowledge of Chinese countryside cooking with its flavorful and wholesome recipes that would be with them for the rest of their lives.

"I want to stay in the countryside," says this 1973 poster. But in the end, very few did.

A Chronology of the Cultural Revolution

1949	**The People's Republic is Established.** Communist forces defeat the Nationalists, who retreat to Taiwan, and Chairman Mao Zedong proclaims the establishment of the People's Republic of China on the China mainland.
1953	**Central Planning and Rationing Begin.** The government begins to monopolize the purchase of grain from the peasants and its distribution in urban areas. Grain rationing is instituted. The first "five-year plan" for the economy is implemented.
1956	**Collectivization of Agriculture Begins.** Private industry is nationalized. Central planning is in full gear. Agricultural cooperatives are formed.
1958	**The Great Leap Forward is Launched.** Mao launches the movement to speed economic development. Communes are established in rural areas, and kitchens are banned in private households in many areas. Local officials dramatically exaggerate productivity in official reports and force peasants to sell all they have to the government.
1959	**Nationwide Famine Begins.** The crisis lasts for three years. As many as 40 million people perish, mostly in rural areas.
1962	**The Government Eases Collectivization.** Peasants are permitted to farm small plots of land privately and sell some produce in open markets. This policy, promoted by Party moderates like Liu Shaoqi and Deng Xiaoping, boosts productivity immediately. Famine ends, and rigid rationing of food in urban areas is relaxed.
1963	**Dazhai Saves its Harvest.** The Dazhai production brigade in Shanxi Province overcomes a damaging flood and saves its harvest. Dazhai is declared a model agricultural collective.
1964	**Peasants Urged to "Learn from Dazhai."** Mao uses Dazhai to signal his renewed determination to advance collectivization. He also launches a campaign to "purify" the Party in rural areas by purging many officials.
1965	**The "Little Red Book" is Distributed.** *Quotations From Chairman Mao,* published the previous year, is promoted nationwide, signaling new energy behind the Mao cult.
May, 1966	**The Cultural Revolution Begins.** Mao launches the "Great Proletarian Cultural Revolution" on May 16 by urging students to rebel against the "repressive" education system. The true targets, however, are so-called "capitalist roaders" in the Party like Liu Shaoqi and Deng Xiaoping, whom Mao believes still retain "capitalist" ideas.
June-Sept., 1966	**The Red Guards are Established.** Radical students form Red Guard organizations in middle schools and colleges. With Mao's encouragement, they travel around the nation – transportation, food and lodging all paid for by the state – destroying the so-called "Four Olds": old ideas, old culture, old customs and old habits. Millions of teachers and alleged "class enemies" are incarcerated, publicly humiliated and brutally tortured. Schools cease to hold classes.

Oct., 1966	**"Capitalist Reactionaries" are Exposed.** Mao reveals his true targets at a Party Central Committee meeting. Liu Shaoqi and Deng Xiaoping are accused of spearheading a "capitalist reactionary line." Mao urges workers and students to join the fight.
Jan – June, 1967	**Mass Organizations Seize Power.** Mao urges the masses to seize power from local "capitalist roaders." The mass organizations divide into opposing factions and attempt to grab power. As the nation sinks into chaos, military forces move in to keep order, but Mao intervenes to thwart them.
June, 1967	**Local Civil Wars Break Out.** Violent conflict ensues among mass organizations. They seize weapons from the military, which is ordered by Mao and his cohorts not to resist. Local civil wars are fought in Mao's name. Many factories are closed and rural areas are also affected, causing a severe shortage of food and consumer goods.
1968	**"Loyalty" Campaign Begins.** Civil war continues and spreads to many areas. Lin Biao, Mao's right-hand man, launches a "loyalty" campaign," and nearly everyone sports Mao buttons in public. Food rationing intensifies.
July-Oct. 1968	**Worker Propaganda Teams Restore Order.** Mao sends worker-led propaganda teams to the schools to attempt to restore order, followed by the military. Mass organizations are dissolved. Those who resist military rule are arrested, and many are executed.
Dec., 1968	**City Youth "Sent Down" to the Countryside.** Mao instructs high school students to resettle in the countryside, easing political tension and solving an unemployment problem in urban areas. From 1968-1977, 17 million city youth are sent to rural areas, as are most teachers and government officials. Urban administrative duties are left to the military.
Mar., 1969	**China Clashes with the Soviets.** Chinese and Russian armies clash in border skirmishes, marking further deterioration in the bilateral relationship with the Soviet Union.
Apr., 1969	**Lin Biao Promoted; Liu Shaoqi Purged.** The Communist Party holds its Ninth Congress and names Lin Biao Mao's successor. Lin proclaims the "overall great victory" of the Cultural Revolution. The Party also officially expels Liu Shaoqi, who dies in jail a few months later.
1970	**"Counterrevolutionaries" Attacked.** The "One-Strike, Three-Antis" campaign is launched to suppress "rebellious elements." Millions of alleged "counterrevolutionaries" are arrested and executed.
July, 1971	**Kissinger Visits China.** U.S. National Security Adviser Henry Kissinger secretly visits China, paving the way for a visit by President Richard M. Nixon the following year.
Sept., 1971	**Lin Biao Dies After Coup.** Lin Biao is killed in a plane crash in Mongolia, allegedly in the act of fleeing to the Soviet Union after a failed coup and an aborted plan to assassinate Mao. He is vilified by the Party.
Feb., 1972	**Nixon Visits China.** U.S. President Richard M. Nixon visits China and meets Mao and Premier Zhou Enlai. The two nations sign the Shanghai Communiqué, pledging to work toward normalization of relations.

1972-1973	**Moderates Return to Power.** The military retreats from civilian life, and many purged government officials return to assume power. Among them is Deng Xiaoping, again appointed Vice Premier. Food shortage continues, as does rigid rationing.
1974	**Moderate Policies Attacked.** Mao launches the "Criticize Lin Biao and Confucius" campaign, an attack on moderate policies. Premier Zhou falls ill with cancer, and Deng Xiaoping is put in charge of the economy.
Jan., 1976	**Zhou Enlai Dies.** Premier Zhou Enlai, a beloved symbol of political moderation, dies of cancer. Hua Guofeng is named Acting Premier the following month.
Apr., 1976	**Jiang Qing Criticized; Deng Xiaoping Purged.** Mourners gather in cities to honor Zhou. Their spontaneous activities turn into demonstrations. Protesters denounce Mao's wife, Jiang Qing, a symbol of radicalism, and her cohorts. The government sends in armed militias and thousands are arrested. Deng Xiaoping is accused of instigating the resistance movement and is purged a second time.
Sept., 1976	**Hua Guofeng Ascends; Mao Dies.** Mao allegedly tells Hua Guofeng, "With you in charge, my heart is at ease." Mao dies on September 9 at the age of 83.
Oct., 1976	**The "Gang of Four" is Arrested.** Less than a month after Mao's death, Hua Guofeng, supported by the military, arrests Jiang Qing and three other radical Party leaders. The fall of the so-called "Gang of Four," as they were called, signals the end of the Mao era.
July, 1977	**Deng Xiaoping Returns to Power.** He soon becomes China's undisputed paramount leader, although he does not assume any additional titles at this time.
Sept., 1977	**University Examinations Restored.** Deng orders the restoration of college entrance examinations, for which all sent-down youth are declared eligible. 5.7 million young people take the exam, and 300,000 are admitted to universities. The youth are permitted to return to urban areas; most do.
1978	**Collectivization is Reversed.** Peasants in some rural areas spontaneously begin to divide up collectivized land and return to family farming. The new "household responsibility system" immediately boosts food production. The government begins to relax food rationing.
Dec., 1978	**Cultural Revolution is Condemned.** The 11th Communist Party Congress, in its Third Plenum, declares the Cultural Revolution to have been a great blunder. The Party leadership vows to focus on modernizing the economy.
Jan., 1979	**U.S. and China Establish Diplomatic Ties.** After 30 years of estrangement, the People's Republic of China and the United States of America establish full diplomatic relations. Embassies are set up in both capitals.
1979	**Agricultural Reform Launched.** The Communist Party officially launches agricultural reform. Rural collectivization is abandoned completely. The food rationing system continues for a few more years, but tapers off and ends in the 1990s.

Some Utensils You'll Need

A rural Chinese kitchen was – and still is – a fairly basic affair. The key pieces of equipment are a large, cast iron wok; an iron spatula; some pots for boiling water, cooking soup and boiling rice; a ladle; a bamboo steamer; a cutting board; a cleaver; and sometimes a large pair of chopsticks. Here's what you will need in your own kitchen to make the dishes in this book:

- **A wok**, a round-bottomed, metal cooking vessel with one or two handles. Many of today's woks come with a non-stick coating, which makes cleanup easier. Woks are made for cooking on open flames, however, so if you happen to be cooking on an electric stove, you may find it easier to use a flat-bottomed skillet, which will heat more evenly on an electric burner. The wok or skillet should also have a lid that fits it tightly.
- **A stock pot** for boiling water and making soup. It is also useful for boiling rice, and was used for that in the countryside during the Cultural Revolution, but nowadays an electric rice cooker is more efficient for this task, and quite common in China. For some dishes, a clay pot is a better bet, because clay holds heat much better than metal. And an electric slow cooker also does a good job for others, such as *Braised Pork in Soy Sauce*, Chairman Mao's favorite dish (*page 67*).

- **A steamer** of one sort or another. The Chinese use circular bamboo frames with slotted bottoms and a domed lid for many of their steaming needs, but this is not required. You can use a wok to steam if you arrange for the food to sit above, and not in, the water. In a pinch, two chopsticks can be placed horizontally on opposite sides of a wok to create a "platform" to hold a plate or bowl on which the food being steamed is placed. A modern, Western-style steamer does the job equally well.
- **A spatula** to use with the wok. Chinese spatulas are shaped like small shovels and are very efficient at stir-frying and transferring food, but any old spatula can be pressed into service.
- **A cutting board** for slicing and chopping food. Wooden boards are traditional, but many boards today are made of composite material that does not absorb juices, which makes them somewhat more sanitary and easier to keep clean.
- **A sharp knife** for slicing and chopping. Chinese peasants generally use a metal cleaver, but whatever gets the job done is fine.

On Portions, Menus and Table Settings

Portions

Because Chinese food is eaten family-style, usually with several diners helping themselves from common dishes in the middle of the table, it doesn't make a lot of sense to speak of individual dishes in terms of portions, and we have not included such information with the recipes. Rather, Chinese cooks usually plan in terms of number of diners *vs.* number of dishes, and there is a strong preference for putting an even number of entrées on the table, since even numbers are considered luckier than odd ones. So here's a rule of thumb (but not a hard and fast commandment):

- For two diners, make two dishes (plus rice, of course, unless one of the dishes is a rice or noodle dish).
- For three, four or five diners, prepare four dishes.
- For six or seven diners, six dishes.
- For eight or nine diners, eight dishes.
- For 10 or more diners, eight or 10 dishes.

Menus

Since you will probably serve several dishes at any given meal, the question arises as to how to choose them. Generally speaking, you'll want to create a meal with both sufficient protein and a healthy complement of vegetables, and you won't want any two dishes to be too similar. Use a variety of proteins – *e.g.*, meats, seafood and bean curd – and try to include at least one dish that features a green, leafy vegetable. While it is not a cardinal sin to serve, say, two pork dishes at one meal, if you do, make sure they don't taste or look alike. The best meals balance meat, vegetables and seafood, and don't use too much of any one ingredient.

Table Settings

In the countryside, a place setting consisted of a rice bowl, a spoon and a pair of chopsticks. Period. Large, flat plates are for serving common dishes in Chinese cuisine; they are not used in individual place settings. The same is true for large bowls. A set of Chinese banquet dishes might well consist of plates of several sizes, rice bowls, serving spoons (or soup spoons) and chopstick rests, all made out of porcelain. But these would have been for rich people and not used by country cooks. Your American guests might appreciate plates as well as rice bowls, but strictly speaking, all that is necessary is a rice bowl, a spoon and a pair of chopsticks, plus, of course, a napkin.

Vegetables and Tofu

蔬菜与豆腐类

"Magical basin filled with treasures," 1962.

醋溜白菜

Vinegar-Glazed Chinese Cabbage

Ingredients

1 small head of Napa cabbage
3 cloves of garlic
1 Tbsp. (15 g.) cornstarch
2 Tbsp. (30 ml.) cold water

4 Tbsp. (60 ml.) cooking oil
3 Tbsp. (45 ml.) dark vinegar
Dash of salt

This dish is most common in north China, where cabbage enjoys a longer growing season. It is best when made with dark vinegar. Even balsamic vinegar, which is not native to China, gives it a wonderful flavor.

Rinse the cabbage thoroughly and remove any brown leaves. Slice the leaves in half lengthwise and then crosswise into shreds that are approximately 3-4 inches (7-10 cm.) long.

Slice the garlic into thin pieces. Combine the cornstarch and the cold water (it must be cold to avoid lumps) and make a smooth paste.

Heat the oil in a wok until it just begins to smoke. Then add the garlic and stir-fry for 10-15 seconds.

Add the cabbage and stir-fry for about two minutes, until it has softened completely. Add the vinegar and salt and stir-fry for 10 more seconds until it is completely mixed. Then add the cornstarch mix and continue to cook. The liquid will thicken quickly. Transfer to a platter and serve.

"The East is Red" and Cabbage Hearts

Scene from the 1965 movie "The East is Red."

The signature tune of the Cultural Revolution, "The East is Red," got its start as a peasant love song about, of all things, cabbage hearts. The traditional lyrics told of daily life in the countryside. In the 1930s, however, the ditty was pressed into service with new words as a patriotic call to action against Japanese invaders. Then, in 1944, a leftist schoolteacher named Li Mianqi penned yet another set of lyrics, praising Chairman Mao and his devotion to the people.

Li's obsequiousness never paid off. In the service of political correctness, the Party attributed the lyrics to a peasant singer named Li Youyuan, and when Li Mianqi claimed credit during the Cultural Revolution he was denounced.

蘑菇豆腐

Tofu with Mushrooms

Ingredients

2 cups (100 g.) fresh mushrooms
1 cake firm tofu (bean curd)
2 cloves garlic
6 Tbsp. (90 ml.) cooking oil

4 Tbsp. (60 ml.) rice wine (but any wine will do)
3 Tbsp. (45 ml.) soy sauce
1 Tbsp. (12.5 g.) sugar

Bean curd – tofu – does not have much taste of its own; it absorbs flavors from other ingredients. Chinese cooks thus try to use the tastiest mushrooms for this dish. Feel free to experiment with varieties other than white mushrooms.

Slice the mushrooms into ¼-inch thick slices. Slice the bean curd into 10-12 pieces, each about one inch square and ½ inch thick. Don't slice it any thinner than this or it will be prone to fall apart.

Crush the garlic. Heat the oil in a wok over a high flame until it smokes. Add the bean curd and fry it on one side until it browns, about 2-3 minutes. Then turn it over and brown the other side.

Add the garlic, mushrooms, wine, soy sauce and sugar, all on top of the bean curd. Do not stir. Turn the heat down to medium and cover the wok tightly.

After five minutes, remove the cover and stir the ingredients. Then, after 20 seconds, remove and serve.

Black Market Mushrooms

Only three feature films were made during the Cultural Revolution, all with revolutionary themes. "Green Pine Mountain," filmed in 1974 in Hebei Province, told how members of a production team promoted socialism by stopping peasants from focusing on small, private plots. In one scene, a peasant was denounced for gathering mushrooms and selling them illegally on the black market.

While the movie was being filmed, local peasants, who depended on the black market to make ends meet, marched on the set and protested the theme to the film's directors. They feared the movie would spur a political campaign to stop the practice entirely. The film went on to broad distribution, but there is no record that a crackdown ever occurred.

清炒土豆丝

Shallow-Fried Potato Shreds

Ingredients

2 medium potatoes
1 scallion (spring onion)
4 Tbsp. (60 ml.) cooking oil
2-3 cloves garlic

1 whole dried chili pepper
  (optional)
3 tsp. (15 ml.) vinegar
Dash of soy sauce

This dish beats Western-style hash browns in a walk. It's the vinegar that makes all the difference. It is at its best and crunchiest if low-starch, red-skinned potatoes are used.

Scrub the potatoes well and cut them into thin (¼ inch, or 6 mm.) slices and then into matchsticks; it is not necessary to peel them, and Chinese peasants do not do so. Soak the potato shreds in cold water for 10 minutes to remove the surface starch and then drain, rinse and pat dry.

Shred the scallion into pieces of about the same size as the potato sticks and crush the garlic.

In a wok, heat the oil until it just begins to smoke. Add the garlic and stir-fry until it starts to brown. Add the scallion (and chili pepper, if desired) and fry for another 15-30 seconds. Then add the potatoes and continue to stir-fry.

Once the potatoes are warm, add the vinegar and continue to cook until it is absorbed (about a minute). Add the soy sauce and stir-fry for another 2-3 minutes. Transfer to a dish and serve.

Variation: This dish is sometimes made with green pepper. If desired, the pepper should be cut into pieces the same size as the potatoes, added to the wok after the garlic, and fried for about a minute before the scallion is added.

Khrushchev and "Goulash Communism"

In the 1950s, Nikita Khrushchev was more willing than Josef Stalin, his predecessor, to permit limited freedoms in Russia and Eastern Europe. "If we promise only revolution," Khrushchev famously remarked, "they'd ask if it's not better just to have good goulash."

This quip gave rise to what became known as "goulash communism," and gave Mao an opening to criticize Khrushchev for retreating from communist orthodoxy. It also gave a headache to Chinese translators, who, lacking a word for "goulash," settled on "potato and beef stew." Beef was scarce in China in the 1960s, so goulash was not really much of an option. But everyone enjoyed fried potato shreds.

小葱拌豆腐

Tofu with Scallions and Sesame Dressing

Ingredients

1 scallion
1 cake firm tofu (bean curd)

2 tsp. sesame oil
Pinch of salt

Tofu was invented in 164 B.C. by a Chinese nobleman trying to make medicine, and it has taken its rightful place as a major source of protein in the Chinese diet. This amazingly simple dish is incredibly tasty, low in fat and high in protein. Use a firm bean curd to make it, because it will hold its shape better that way.

Shred the scallion into very small pieces, cutting it on the bias to maximize surface area. Rinse the tofu and place it on a microwave-safe serving plate. Warm it by microwaving it on high for one minute, or simply heating it very gently in a conventional oven.

Remove the tofu from the oven and, with a sharp knife or cleaver, cut it up into small pieces about 1½ inches (4 cm.) long, an inch (2.5 cm.) wide and ½ inch (about 1.5 cm.) thick.

Sprinkle the scallion, sesame oil and salt on top of the tofu pieces and serve while still warm.

Note: Obviously there were no microwaves in the Chinese countryside during the Cultural Revolution, nor did peasants have convection ovens. They would simply have soaked the tofu – which would have been freshly made – in hot water for 10 minutes to heat it up.

As Clear as Tofu and Scallions

"Supreme Instruction: 'Struggle against selfishness and criticize revisionism.' "

During the Cultural Revolution, people were often accused of offenses, from stealing or engaging in extramarital affairs to slacking off or having "bad thoughts." Meetings of village production teams were forums for dispute resolution where people were often compelled to criticize themselves or defend themselves against such accusations. A good defense was to proclaim one's loyalty and demonstrate knowledge of communist doctrine, with whatever rhetorical flourishes one could muster.

This dish – its milky white bean curd a sharp contrast to the deep green of its scallions – provided a useful metaphor. If your innocence was "as clear as tofu and scallions," then anyone ought to be able to appreciate it.

干煸四季豆

Dry-Fried Green Beans

Ingredients

1 lb. (450 g.) string beans (French beans)
1 clove garlic
¼ cup (60 ml.) cooking oil
2 Tbsp. (30 ml.) oyster sauce (or, if unavailable, 3 Tbsp. or 45 ml. of soy sauce plus ½ tsp. or 2 g. of sugar, microwaved for 10-15 seconds)

If you eat this dish in a Chinese restaurant today, it's likely to be made with ground pork. Pork was hard to get during the Cultural Revolution, but it gives the dish a great taste. If you want to use it, stir-fry about an eighth of a pound of ground pork separately and add it in at the end.

Snip off the edges of the beans (on both sides) and remove the string from each bean. There is no need to cut the beans in half; they may be used whole in this dish. Crush the garlic.

Heat half the oil in a wok until it is very hot; you'll see a lot of smoke. Add half of the string beans and cook them until they are soft and crinkly, stirring occasionally. Then add half of the garlic and cook for 10 more seconds. Remove from the wok.

Add the rest of the oil to the wok and wait until it heats up. When the oil is smoking, add the rest of the green beans and repeat the steps above, adding garlic at the very end.

Remove from the wok and combine with the first batch of beans. Drizzle with either the oyster sauce or the soy sauce and sugar mixture and serve.

The Chairman's 67th Birthday

"May Chairman Mao live a boundless life of 10,000 years."

China experienced its worst famine beginning in 1959, and Mao announced that he would give up meat, fish and eggs and would eat only the adult male ration of grain, 25-32 catties (27-35 lbs. or 12-16 kg.) a month. When he turned 67 in December of 1960, however, he marked the occasion with a small, private birthday party. Only Mao, his aides and military guards attended.

Years later it became known that the Chairman did not hold himself to his public vow that day. The guests at the celebration feasted on fish head soup, lamb and scallions, dry-fried green beans, cooked greens, fried dried fish and pickled mustard greens.

松子玉米

Stir-Fried Corn and Pine Nuts

Ingredients

2 ears of corn on the cob (or 2 cups – 328 g. – of canned or frozen corn kernels)

1 scallion (spring onion)

½ cup (70 g.) pine nuts
2 Tbsp. (30 ml.) cooking oil
Pinch of salt

Corn was considered low-class, coarse food during the Cultural Revolution, in large part because Chinese corn was far less sweet than today's American variety. The occasional ear of sweet corn that appeared was highly prized and used in dishes like this one.

Place the two ears of corn in their husks in a microwave oven. If the corn has already been husked, wrap it in a wet paper towel first. Microwave for three minutes on high. Remove the husks and silk, or the paper towel, and allow to cool. Then cut the kernels off of the cobs. (If you are using frozen corn, just let it thaw until it is at room temperature; canned corn may be used right out of the can).

Slice the scallion on the bias into small pieces about the same size as the corn kernels.

Place a wok over medium flame and add pine nuts without using any oil. Stir-fry them for a minute until they turn slightly brownish, then remove them from the wok and set them aside.

Add oil to the wok and heat it until it just begins to smoke. Add the scallion pieces and stir-fry very briefly – 10 seconds is enough. Then add the corn and stir-fry for 30 seconds more. Add salt and then return the pine nuts to the wok. Make sure the ingredients are well-mixed and warm. Remove and serve.

"Iron Maiden Teams"

"If the seeds are well-selected, the harvest will be more abundant every year," 1964.

When a flood nearly destroyed the corn crop at the Dazhai production brigade in Shanxi Province in 1963, a 17 year-old girl named Guo Fenglian organized an "iron maiden team" to replant the uprooted stalks. Guo became an icon after that, and Mao proclaimed that in agriculture, the country should learn from Dazhai. Afterwards, brigades throughout the country organized "iron maiden teams" of their own.

大蒜炒菠菜

Stir-Fried Spinach with Garlic

Ingredients

5-6 cloves garlic	1 bunch raw spinach, well-washed
4 tsp. (20 ml.) cooking oil	Dash of salt

Forget about the tasteless, cooked spinach you find in the frozen foods section of the supermarket. This simple, elegant dish is really nothing like it – it is quick, easy and especially delicious. Garlic is the secret – the Chinese often use it to cook leafy vegetables because it adds a lot of flavor.

Crush the garlic or slice it into very small pieces. Then heat the oil in a wok until it begins to smoke heavily. Add the garlic and stir-fry briefly – 10 seconds or so is enough; don't allow it to brown.

Add the spinach and stir-fry. It will reduce in volume considerably, and very quickly. After about 20-30 seconds, remove it from the wok and pour off the excess liquid.

Sprinkle with salt and serve.

A Politically Correct Spinach Purchase

More than 5 billion copies of the *Quotations From Chairman Mao* were printed during the Cultural Revolution, and all actions were justified by quoting from the "little red book." The Chinese had not completely lost their sense of humor, however, and a popular joke imagined buying spinach this way:

Customer: "Chairman Mao's Supreme Instruction: One must save resources for the revolution. I need two catties of spinach."

Sales clerk: "Supreme Instruction of Chairman Mao: One must serve the people. Here is your spinach."

辣味凉拌萝卜

Spicy White Radish Salad

Ingredients

1 large white, Daikon radish (if unavailable, 2-3 turnips may be substituted)

3-4 cloves of garlic

1 slice ginger (about the size and thickness of a quarter)

1 tsp. (5 ml.) vegetable oil

2 Tbsp. (30 ml.) sesame oil

3 Tbsp. (45 ml.) soy sauce

3 Tbsp. (45 ml.) dark vinegar (but white will do)

1 tsp. – 1 Tbsp. (5 – 15 ml.) hot sauce, to taste (Chinese cooks use a paste made with hot peppers, but Tabasco sauce may be substituted)

The Chinese seldom eat vegetables that have not been cooked thoroughly, but this one is an exception. These large radishes – which you can often find in American supermarkets – are especially sweet and lend themselves to being eaten raw. Topping this dish off with a large spoonful of crushed, roasted nuts will add even more flavor and texture.

Wash and peel the radish and slice it into strips about 2-3 inches (5-7 cm.) long and ¼ inch (6mm.) wide. Crush the garlic and chop the ginger, mixing them together into a smooth paste.

Mix all the ingredients (except the radish) together and add them to the garlic-ginger paste. Blend them well into a sauce.

Arrange the radish pieces on a serving plate, cover with the sauce and serve.

The Emperor's New Bike

Pu Yi in jail, writing a self-criticism.

China's last Emperor, Pu Yi, who had been deposed in 1912, was sent to a labor camp during the Cultural Revolution with some former Nationalist officials. Not fit to work in the fields, they were assigned kitchen duty. They had to transport vegetables in a bicycle-propelled flatbed truck.

Pu Yi, who had had a bike as a child, knew how to ride it, but four huge baskets of radishes, potatoes and tomatoes proved too much for him. One day he lost control and found himself lying on the ground, covered with vegetables. He took it all good-naturedly, though. Recalling his riding days in the Forbidden City, he quipped that he was now using "a much bigger tricycle in a much bigger world."

香菇葫芦瓜

Squash with Shiitake Mushrooms

Ingredients

5 dried shiitake mushrooms
2 medium-sized squash (or 3 of
   the smaller Asian variety, if
   available)
1 scallion (spring onion)

2 tsp. (10 ml.) cold water
1 tsp. (6 g.) cornstarch
2 tsp. (10 ml.) cooking oil
Dash of salt
½ tsp. (2 g.) sugar

Dried shiitake mushrooms taste very different from fresh ones and are far more flavorful, but must be reconstituted before being cooked. Fresh ones can, however, be used in a pinch in this dish.

Soak the dried mushrooms in hot water for half an hour until they are soft.

Slice the squash diagonally into slivers about 2-3 inches (5-7 cm.) long and 1/8 inch (3 mm.) thick. No need to remove the skin. Slice the scallion in the same way. Squeeze out the mushrooms (reserving the liquid) and slice them into pieces about the same size as the squash, discarding the hard stems and using only the soft caps. Mix the water and cornstarch to form a paste, taking care to work out any lumps.

Heat the oil in a wok until it smokes. Add the scallion and stir-fry briefly. Then add the squash and cook for 30 seconds. Add the mushrooms and the liquid in which they were soaked. Then cover the wok and cook for two minutes over medium heat.

Add the salt and sugar and the cornstarch mixture. Stir briefly until the liquid thickens. Remove and serve.

Communists Are "Squash on the Vine"

"Huge pumpkin," 1964.

After the famine of 1959, many wanted the commune system banned. The leftists, however wanted to preserve it, and promoted it with a popular ditty comparing communes to vines:

*"The commune is an ever-green vine
The members are squash on the vine
The squash and the vine are connected
The healthier the vine, the bigger the squash."*

In 1962, Mao heard the song and proclaimed, "We must insist on promoting the people's communes. People should share in the difficulties as well as the happiness." And share they did.

麻婆豆腐

Old Pockmarked Granny's Tofu

Ingredients

1 cake firm tofu (bean curd)
3-4 cloves garlic
1 scallion (spring onion), or
  a small bunch of cilantro
  (coriander) or parsley for
  garnish
1 tsp. (6 g.) cornstarch
2 tsp. (10 ml.) cold water

2 Tbsp. (30 ml.) cooking oil
2-3 hot whole chili peppers
  (dried)
½ tsp. (1.5 g.) black pepper
1 Tbsp.(15 ml.) sesame oil
1 tsp. (4 g.) sugar
2 Tbsp. (30 ml.) soy sauce

In China, this recipe calls for chilies and black pepper, but if you prefer things hotter, use whatever type of pepper you like.

Slice the tofu into cubes about one inch (2.5 cm.) on all sides. Crush the garlic and cut the scallion (or cilantro or parsley) into small pieces. Mix the cornstarch and water to form a paste, removing any lumps. Then heat the wok and add the cooking oil. When it begins to smoke, add the garlic and the whole chili peppers. (Cutting them up will make the dish considerably spicier). Fry briefly for about 10 seconds and then add the sugar and soy sauce. Fry for another 10 seconds and add the tofu.

Make sure the tofu is coated with the mixture, and then let it sit over a medium flame for 2-3 minutes until it is heated through. Do not move it excessively. Add the black pepper, sesame oil and cornstarch paste and mix well. Remove from the wok, garnish and serve.

Note: Adding ground pork to this dish makes it particularly flavorful. Use about 1/8 lb. of ground pork and stir-fry it with the garlic and chili peppers.

Signs of the Times

"Old Pockmarked Granny Chen's Bean Curd."

For more than a century, a sign hung over the entrance of a Beijing restaurant called "Old Pockmarked Granny Chen's Bean Curd Restaurant." In 1966, however, some of the establishment's employees argued that because Granny Chen had been a capitalist, a socialist enterprise should not use her name.

Nobody dared argue, so they pulled the sign down and hacked it to pieces with cleavers. To avoid any vestiges of capitalism, they then changed the name of the signature dish to "numbing and spicy bean curd," which sounded quite close to the original name in Chinese. After the Cultural Revolution, however, the names of both the restaurant and its most famous dish were restored, and the establishment still does business in Beijing's western district today.

锅塌豆腐

Pan-Fried Tofu in a Light Sauce

Ingredients

1 cake firm tofu (bean curd)

4 tsp. (20 ml.) cooking oil

1 small cube of ginger, about ½
  inch (1.5 cm.) on each side

2 Tbsp. (15 ml.) soy sauce

1 Tbsp. (12 g.) sugar

2 eggs (optional)

2 scallions (spring onion)

Even firm tofu contains a lot of water, so when frying it, make sure most of the liquid evaporates. This allows other flavors to work their way in and permeate the tofu.

Slice the tofu into rectangles approximately three inches (7 cm.) long, two inches (5 cm.) wide and ½ inch (1.5 cm.) thick. Then add the oil to a flat-bottomed frying pan and place it over medium heat. Crush the ginger.

Before the oil begins to smoke, place the tofu pieces flat on the bottom of the pan, trying to avoid breaking them. Fry for 5-7 minutes; they will begin to release their water. When the bottom surface of the tofu begins to brown, turn the pieces over carefully and fry the other sides. Do this only once; the tofu is fragile and should not be moved excessively.

When the second side begins to brown, add the soy sauce, sugar and ginger, and cover the pot tightly for a full minute. In the meantime, beat the two eggs together.

Remove the cover and add the beaten eggs (if desired), and the scallions. Allow the eggs to cook – this will take only about a half a minute or so. Carefully transfer to a serving plate.

Supreme Instructions on Bean Curd

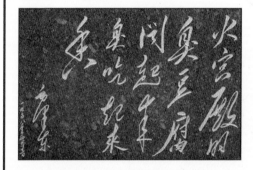

An endorsement of Huogongdian's bean curd in the Chairman's own calligraphy.

Quotes from Chairman Mao decorated the walls of every public place during the Cultural Revolution, painted in huge characters. Most were from the "little red book," but any words Mao uttered were considered fair game.

In 1958, Mao returned to his native Hunan Province and visited Huogongdian, a famous restaurant in the city of Changsha. He ordered an infamous bean curd dish he had enjoyed there as a young man, discovered that it was as tasty as ever, and happily proclaimed it so. The staff recognized a good opportunity when they saw it. After Mao's visit they painted his quote on the wall: "The strong-smelling bean curd at Huogongdian smells foul, but tastes delicious."

鱼香茄子

Braised Eggplant with Minced Pork

Ingredients

1-2 eggplants, or aubergines (1 if you use the American kind, but 2 if it's the Chinese variety)
10 cloves garlic
1 scallion (spring onion)
4 Tbsp. (60 ml.) cooking oil

½ lb. (225 g.) ground pork
2 Tbsp. (30 ml.) oyster sauce (or soy sauce, if unavailable)
1 tsp. (4 g.) sugar
1 tsp. (5 ml.) sesame oil

Chinese eggplant – long, thin and cucumber-shaped – is a far cry from the large, meaty, pear-shaped American variety. Either type works in this dish, however.

Slice the eggplant in half lengthwise. Score each half diagonally, through the skin, taking care not to slice all the way through. Then make perpendicular scores so the ultimate effect is one of cross-hatching. Cut it into pieces about a half an inch (1.5 cm.) thick and two inches (5 cm.) long.

Place the eggplant pieces on a serving plate and microwave on high for eight minutes. (This dish is traditionally deep fried, but microwaving saves time and a lot of calories).

Crush the garlic and slice the scallion into half-inch lengths. Heat a wok and add the oil. When it is hot but not yet smoking, add the garlic and stir-fry until fragrant. Add the ground pork and scallion and continue cooking until the pork changes color completely.

Add the oyster sauce (or soy) sauce and sugar and stir-fry until most of the liquid in the wok has been absorbed or has evaporated. Pour the mixture over the eggplant. Remove from the wok, sprinkle with sesame oil and serve.

Anything but Abundant

"The vegetables are green, the melons plump and the yield abundant," 1959.

The poster above, which predates the Cultural Revolution by a few years, is rich in irony. It depicts a plentiful harvest of melons, eggplant, cucumbers, potatoes, tomatoes, corn and onions at precisely the time when the reality was quite the opposite. As Mao's "Great Leap Forward" mandated that peasants abandon private farming, reorganize into communes and adopt a host of politically correct but impractical farming techniques, the Chinese countryside plunged headlong into famine and desperation. Sadly, the yield, in 1959, was anything but abundant.

甜酸萝卜

44

Sweet and Sour White Radish

Ingredients

½ large white Daikon radish
(but a couple of garden-variety
turnips can be substituted)

Enough white vinegar to cover
the radish (after it is sliced)
5-6 Tbsp. (60-70 g.) sugar

Appetizers are uncommon in the Chinese countryside, but there is a general consensus that the combination of sweet and sour tastes that characterize dishes like this stimulate the appetite. This same basic process can be applied to many other vegetables, such as carrots, cabbage, string beans and cucumbers.

Wash and peel the radish and cut it into shreds about 2-3 inches (5-7 cm.) long. Then place the pieces in a large bowl and add enough vinegar to cover them.

Add the sugar and let marinate for at least 15 minutes. Serve at room temperature or refrigerate and serve cold. This dish only gets better over time; it can stay in the refrigerator for three to four days. Use it as a cold appetizer before a meal.

Destroying An Old Sign

The sign that hung over Liu Biju – a Beijing pickling house famous for preserved radishes, cucumbers, cabbage and garlic – dated from the Ming Dynasty and survived into the twentieth century. Red Guards carried it off during the Cultural Revolution as part of the campaign to destroy the "Four Olds," but it was not damaged. It was eventually returned to the shop after the madness was over.

辣白菜

Spicy Pickled Cabbage

Ingredients

4-5 leaves Napa cabbage (leaves from the heart are best)

2-3 chili peppers (dried)

1/3 cup (80 ml.) white vinegar

4 Tbsp. (50 g.) sugar

Dash of salt

This is one of those dishes you find virtually everywhere in China. Even when vegetables were scarce, a little of this dish added just enough flavor to help the rice – or other bland, starchy food like steamed bread – go down. Chinese cooks sometimes also stir-fry pickled cabbage with pork or fish.

Boil about four cups (1 liter) of water in a pot and after it reaches a rolling boil, place the cabbage leaves in it for about five seconds. They should soften a bit but still retain some crispness. Remove and cut the leaves in pieces about an inch (2.5 cm.) square. Then drain and cool.

Cut the chili peppers into small pieces. Discard the seeds if you want the dish to be mild; retain them if you prefer it hotter. Combine with the other ingredients in a large bowl.

Add the cabbage and mix well. Let it sit for a half hour and then serve at room temperature.

Centrally Planned Cabbage

"Ensure the supply of vegetables to the urban areas," 1950s.

Central planning, a Soviet import, meant that China's government decided which crops to grow and where to plant them. The bureaucrats made many poor decisions, but the order to decrease celery, tomato and pepper cultivation in north China and focus on boosting cabbage production made sense. The strain of cabbage developed in Inner Mongolia had two advantages: a short growing season and the ability to withstand frost and last half a year without preservation. As a result, Chinese in the north had vegetables all winter, and could eat any vegetable they chose – as long as it was cabbage.

Poultry

鸡鸭类

"Strong hens lay more eggs," 1978.

蜂蜜红焖鸭子

Honey Braised Duck

Ingredients

1 Tbsp. (15 ml.) cooking oil
1 large piece ginger (about 1 inch, or 2.5 cm., on each side)
1 whole duckling
3-4 Tbsp. (45-60 ml.) honey
½ cup (120 ml.) rice wine (but any wine will do)
6-7 Tbsp. (about 100 ml.) soy sauce (dark soy sauce is best for this dish)
4 scallions (spring onions)

Although some restaurants in China used ovens to roast duck, virtually no Chinese homes possessed them during the Cultural Revolution. This dish, made in a wok, served as a wonderful stand-in for the roasted variety.

Heat a wok and add oil. Crush the ginger. Before the oil begins to smoke, add the ginger to the wok and fry it for a minute so its flavor permeates the oil.

Add the entire duckling to the wok and fry one side over a high flame for about 10 minutes until the skin tightens and turns brownish. Then turn it over and fry the other side for 10 minutes. Add the honey, wine and soy sauce and place two whole scallions on either side of the duck and two in the duck's cavity.

Cover the wok tightly and turn the heat down to medium. Allow the duck to braise for about an hour and a half for a three-pound (1.3 kg.) duckling, or an hour and fifteen minutes for a smaller bird. Turn several times to ensure that the duck is cooked evenly, spooning the liquid over – and inside – the bird.

When the meat is ready to fall off the bones, remove from the wok and serve.

Caring for the Production Team's Ducks

"The experience of herding ducks," 1974.

Young Pioneers, Party-organized groups of children aged 7-14, took care of certain tasks on the farms during the Cultural Revolution. A popular story was told of three such children tasked with caring for ducks by the production team in their village. Their job was to keep the ducks away from the fields.

When some of the ducks escaped and began eating grain, the peasants criticized the children, who also performed self-criticisms of their own, as was the custom during this period. Later, they redeemed themselves by turning in a selfish peasant who had secretly sent his own ducks to eat in the public field.

酱油子鸡

Rock Cornish Game Hen in Soy Sauce

Ingredients

1 small piece ginger (about ½ inch, or 1.5 cm., on a side)

4 Tbsp. (60 ml.) soy sauce

8 Tbsp. (120 ml.) cold water

1 Tbsp. (12 g.) sugar

1 large Rock Cornish game hen

Cornish hens are not native to China, but they are the closest thing you are likely to find in a Western supermarket to the young, immature hens that the cooks prefer to use in Guangdong Province, where this dish originates.

Slice the ginger into small pieces and put it in a saucepan large enough to accommodate the hen. Add the soy sauce, sugar and water. Then heat the mixture until it begins to boil.

Add the whole hen (don't cut it up), Then cover the pot tightly and turn the heat down to medium.

Cook the hen for 10 minutes. After the bottom begins to brown, turn it over to allow the other side to brown, turning the heat down to low. Cover the pot again.

Cook for another 15 minutes. Then turn off the heat, but let the hen sit in the covered pot for an additional 10 minutes.

Cut up the hen as desired and arrange on a serving plate.

Cock-Crow in the Wee Hours

A story published in 1955 that became a cartoon on the eve of the Cultural Revolution concerned a landholder who insisted his farm hands begin work every day at cock-crow. But when it seemed the rooster crowed earlier and earlier as time went on, the hands discovered this hateful landlord was secretly rising in the wee hours to wake the bird. So they set a trap for him one night. Pretending he was a chicken thief, they beat him senseless in the dark night.

The story was used as an object lesson in persecution by landed gentry. But the truth was otherwise. An investigative journalist who visited the village a half century later learned that the landlord was actually a hard-working man who had enjoyed respect in the village before the Communist takeover.

棒棒鸡

Shredded Chicken with Peanut Sauce

Ingredients

2 chicken breasts, boned
Enough water to cover the
   chicken
6 Tbsp. (85 g.) peanut butter
3 Tbsp. (45 ml.) soy sauce
1 Tbsp. (15 ml.) white vinegar

2 Tbsp. (24 g.) sugar
2 Tbsp. (30 ml.) sesame oil
2 Tbsp. (15 g.) cilantro (coriander)
   or scallions (spring onions),
   shredded

In China, this dish is usually made with sesame paste rather than peanut butter, but they work equally well alone or in combination.

Bring a quart of water to a boil in a pot. Drop the chicken breasts in the boiling water and boil them until they are cooked completely through. You may want to check every so often by cutting into one breast to see if the meat is still at all pink. But do not overcook the chicken; once the meat is completely white, remove it from the water immediately and allow it to cool.

When the chicken has cooled down, shred both breasts by hand, pulling off matchstick-sized pieces. You can slice the chicken with a knife if you are in a hurry, but it's not recommended. For this dish, hand-shredding is traditional, and gives a more pleasing texture.

Mix together the peanut butter, soy sauce, vinegar and sugar, and microwave the mixture for about 15 seconds until the peanut butter melts and the mixture is a consistent paste. Then add the sesame oil. Mix the cilantro or scallions with the chicken shreds and arrange on a serving plate. Then pour the sauce on top. Typically, the chicken and sauce are mixed together on the table. Serve cold.

The Hundred Chicken Banquet

Mao's wife, Jiang Qing, asserted control over the Communist Party's leadership of the cultural life of the nation, and by the late 1960s, only eight "model operas," each with a revolutionary theme, were permitted to be performed. One such play, called "Taking Tiger Mountain by Strategy," was based on the true story of a 1946 incident in the Chinese civil war in which a Communist operative in Manchuria disguised himself in order to kill mountain bandits who had been paid by Nationalist forces to destroy the Communists. Posing as a fellow traveler, he infiltrated a birthday banquet given by a local bandit in which 100 chickens were served. He led an attack in which all the guests were killed, and the Communists gained control of the entire region as a result.

姜葱白切鸡

Ginger and Scallion Poached Chicken

Ingredients

1 3-4 lb. (1.3-1.8 kg.) stewing hen
(smaller is better; Cornish hens
work well)

1 medium-sized piece of ginger
root (about ¾ inch, or 2 cm., on

a side)

2 scallions (spring onions)

1 tsp. salt (6 g.)

3 Tbsp. vegetable oil (45 ml.)

*To cooks in Guangdong Province, overcooking this dish is a sin. If
you eat it in a Cantonese restaurant, it is very likely to be served
while the meat is still pink around the bones.*

Heat enough water to cover the chicken in a pot and
bring it to a rolling boil. Add the chicken, cover,
and turn the heat down to low. Don't let the water
return to a boil.

After 15 minutes, turn off the heat and leave the chicken
in the covered pot for another 30 minutes. In the meantime,
chop the ginger and scallions finely. Mix with the salt and
place in a small dish.

Heat the oil in a wok until it begins to smoke and pour it
over the ginger, scallion and salt mix. Remove the chicken
and rinse in cold water. Then cut it into small pieces. Chinese cooks remove the limbs and hack through the bones
so each piece has some skin, some meat and some bone. If
you prefer, however, you can remove the bones and simply
serve the skin and meat.

Serve on a large plate, accompanied by the small dish
of condiments. Diners dip the chicken into the sauces before
eating.

Chickens Coming Home to Roost

"A new look in poultry farms," 1978.

The Cantonese traditionally celebrate
Chinese New Year with a chicken. From
1968-70, food was so scarce in Guangdong Province that each household was
allowed only one fowl per year. Raising
chickens at home thus became common-
place, despite the fact that the average
living space afforded only four square
meters (43 square feet) per person. Apart-
ment-raised chickens were a far more
common sight than the scientific chicken
farm depicted in this 1978 rendering.

汽锅鸡

Steamed Ginger and Mushroom Chicken

Ingredients

5-6 dried shiitake mushrooms
1 large piece ginger, about 1 inch
   (2.5 cm.) on each side
1 lb. (450 g.) chicken thighs
2 Tbsp. (30 ml.) soy sauce

½ Tbsp. (6 g.) sugar
Dash of salt
1 tsp. (6 g.) cornstarch
4 cups (1 liter) water

The Chinese do not use boneless chicken in this dish, but you can do so if you wish. Just be sure to use dark meat; this dish is much less flavorful if white meat is used. In the photo, you can see the special earthenware pot that the Chinese sometimes use for steaming foods as well as some herbal medicines, but note that such pots retain more liquid that simple bowls.

Soak the mushrooms in hot water. Slice the ginger into paper-thin shreds. Cut the chicken into 4-5 pieces, hacking right through the bone. Each piece should be about an inch (2.5 cm.) on each side.

Marinate the chicken with the soy sauce, sugar, salt and cornstarch, making sure that the cornstarch dissolves completely and is not in lumps. Let it sit for at least 15 minutes.

Remove the mushrooms from the water, reserving the liquid. Discard the hard stems and slice the caps into shreds. Place them in a bowl together with the chicken and the ginger. Mix well.

Put about four cups (1 liter) of water in a wok and place the bowl on a steamer rack above it. Set the flame on medium, cover and steam the mixture for 20 minutes – not longer, as this dish should not be overcooked. Remove from the burner and serve.

Building Missiles by Incubating Chicks

After being accused of being a Communist sympathizer and jailed for five years, M.I.T.-educated Qian Xuesen left the United States and returned to his native China, where he headed China's missile program and helped develop the Silkworm missile. Qian's development strategy for China was called "incubating chicks," meaning that rather than promoting individual research, China would develop a generation of scientists to work as a team. That team, set up in 1956, played a crucial role in developing China's first atomic bomb. During the Cultural Revolution, Premier Zhou Enlai protected Qian and his team from harm.

潮州卤水鸭

Stewed Duck Chaozhou Style

Ingredients

5-6 pieces star anise
Large piece of ginger (about 1 inch, or 2.5 cm., on a side)
5-6 whole brown peppercorns
1 stick cinnamon
8-10 whole cloves
4 scallions (spring onions), or one

medium onion
2 cups (500 ml.) soy sauce (dark variety is best)
1 cup (250 ml.) wine, any variety
3 Tbsp. (40 g.) sugar
1 whole duckling

The broth used to make this dish may be saved, frozen and re-used with duck or even tofu or meat. In fact, Chinese cooks prefer to use the same liquid over and over again, sometimes for many years. In the era before refrigeration, stewing food in this way was a common method of preserving it.

Put enough water to cover the duck in a large pot and turn the heat up to high. Add all of the ingredients except the duck and bring to a boil. Then turn the heat down to very low, cover and allow to simmer for one hour.

Turn the heat back up to high and allow to boil a second time. When the liquid reaches a rolling boil, add the whole duck and allow to boil once again.

Cover the pot again and reduce the heat to medium-low. Let cook for about one hour, turning the duck occasionally to permit it to cook evenly. Remove and serve.

"Destroy Privately Owned Ducks"

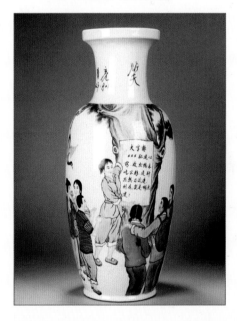

Raising a duck privately was fraught with danger during the Cultural Revolution, since ducks were hard to control and often escaped. The "destroy privately owned ducks" campaign was immortalized on a vase produced in China's porcelain capital, Jingdezhen. It depicts a group of young people who caught a duck feeding on public grain. They hanged the duck on a tree and wrote a large-character poster criticizing the owner.

清蒸嫩鸭子

Steamed Duckling with Ginger

Ingredients

1 whole duckling	(about 1½ inches, or 4 cm., on
1 Tbsp. (20 g.) salt	a side)
½ cup (120 ml.) wine	2 scallions (spring onions)
1 very large piece of ginger	5-6 black or white peppercorns

Chinese wine is traditionally made from rice, and rice wine has a very different flavor from grape wine because it does not contain much sugar. In a pinch you can use either kind in this dish, but look for rice wine first.

Marinate the duckling in the salt and the wine, and let it sit for at least 15 minutes. Smash the ginger but keep it in one piece. Then place it, together with the scallions (whole) and the pepper, in the cavity of the duckling. Place in a roasting pan and cover tightly.

Set your oven to 250°F (120°C or gas mark ½) and place the pan in the cold oven. Let it cook for three and a half hours; there is no need to check it periodically. It is done when the meat is falling off the bones.

Note: Chinese cooks traditionally steam this dish on top of the stove. While this variation uses an oven and a tight seal, the dish can also be prepared in a steamer on the stovetop if you prefer.

"Contradictions" in Collectivization

"A flock of ducks belonging to the cooperative," 1957.

News of the failures of the Great Leap Forward trickled into Beijing in the late 1950s, and by 1959 even Mao had to admit that things were not going as well as planned. In a speech in Zhengzhou in February, he continued to defend collectivization, but acknowledged that the speed at which the communes had been established had resulted in "contradictions." Among them: property, like chickens, ducks and some pigs, had been appropriated without paying the peasants for them. In the end, the disasters caused by the Great Leap would take years to reverse, and would set the stage for Mao's launch of the Cultural Revolution.

Pork

猪肉类

"Energetically develop hog-raising," 1976.

红烧肉

Braised Pork in Soy Sauce

Ingredients

1 lb. (450 g.) pork shoulder
1 large piece ginger, about 1 inch
   (2.5 cm.) on a side
1 Tbsp. (15 ml.) cooking oil
4 Tbsp. (50 g.) sugar
4 Tbsp. (60 ml.) soy sauce

1 cinnamon stick (½ tsp. or 5 g.
   powdered cinnamon may be
   substituted)
½ cup (120 ml.) rice wine (or any
   other wine)

This dish is traditionally made with pork belly, but it's hard to find in many supermarkets and it's far fattier than other cuts. There's enough fat in pork shoulder to give the dish a great taste, and still save a few calories and maybe a hardened artery.

Cut the pork shoulder into cubes, about one inch (2.5 cm.) on each side. Smash the ginger with the side of a cleaver; no need to peel it.

Heat a wok and add the oil. When it begins to smoke, add the ginger and then the sugar. Once the sugar has dissolved completely, add the pork. Stir-fry the mixture until most of the liquid has evaporated, but not until it is completely dry. Then add the soy sauce, cinnamon and wine.

Mix well and then cover the wok tightly. Turn the heat down to medium and let simmer for ½ hour. Remove and serve.

The Chairman's Brain Food

Chairman Mao believed that the fat in Braised Pork in Soy Sauce had the capability to boost his brainpower. The dish is traditionally regarded as brain food in his native Hunan Province, and it was well-known as the Chairman's favorite. In fact, he insisted that his Hunanese chef cook it for him often, even during his years in Beijing and over the strenuous objection of his personal physicians.

Mao was especially fond of eating this dish before he went into combat – either physical or political – and believed he never lost a battle when well-fed on braised pork.

韭菜炒肉丝

Stir-Fried Pork Shreds with Chives

Ingredients

¾ lb. (350 g.) lean pork
2 Tbsp. (30 ml.) soy sauce
1 tsp. (4 g.) sugar
1 tsp. (6 g.) cornstarch (you can
   use flour as a substitute)

5 cloves of garlic
4 Tbsp. (60 ml.) vegetable oil
2 bunches of chives, each the
   diameter of a quarter (or a 2p
   coin)

While this recipe calls for chives, in China the dish is actually made with a kind of Chinese leek that is much thinner than its Western counterpart. Both are cousins of scallions (spring onions) and have the characteristic taste common to this family. You can use either.

Pound the pork with the dull edge of a cleaver (or some other blunt instrument) until it is about ¼ inch (6 mm.) thick; this will help tenderize the meat. Then cut it against the grain into matchstick-sized pieces about an inch and a half (4 cm.) long. Place the pork shreds in a bowl and marinate them in a mixture of the soy sauce, sugar and cornstarch.

Smash the garlic with the side of the cleaver and remove the dry skin. Then chop the crushed garlic into small pieces.

In a wok, heat the oil until it just begins to smoke. Add the garlic and fry until it begins to brown. Then add the pork and stir-fry. When the meat begins to turn color, add the chives and continue to stir-fry until the pork turns completely brown. Remove and serve.

Cutting off the Tail of Capitalism

"Competition in work," 1965.

During the Cultural Revolution, chives were considered the symbolic tail of capitalism. Peasants, who were required to abandon all side occupations, still raised small quantities of their own produce. Chives, which could be grown anywhere in secrecy, grew back very quickly once cut down. This characteristic made them a made-to-order metaphor for "capitalist remnants."

香葱猪肉饼

Minced Pork and Scallion Cake

Ingredients

½ lb. (225 g.) ground pork
2 scallions (spring onions)
2 tsp. soy sauce
1 Tbsp. (12 g.) sugar

1 Tbsp. (15g.) cornstarch
1½ cups (350 ml.) water
Several sprigs of cilantro
(coriander)

This is the closest Chinese equivalent to American meat loaf. Variations include adding chopped shiitake mushrooms and chopped, cooked shrimp. The dish may also be served on a bed of green vegetables or with warmed tofu.

Mix all of the ingredients together thoroughly except for the cilantro. Then press the mixture into the bottom of a heat-safe dish so it takes the shape of the bottom of the dish. Chop the cilantro roughly and mince the scallions.

Boil the water in the bottom of a steamer, or in a wok with some sort of frame that will permit the suspension of a dish above water level. In a pinch, a couple of chopsticks can serve this purpose nicely. The idea is to steam the mixture, making use of the steam from the boiling water.

When the pork is fully cooked and changes color – after 15 minutes or so – remove the hot dish from the wok suspension. Place a plate or a dish upside-down on the top of the dish in which the meat has been steamed and, using potholders, turn the dish upside down so the mixture is transferred to the plate.

Garnish with the chopped cilantro and serve.

The Pig Will Be Healthy Forever

One was supposed to proclaim "long live Chairman Mao" upon seeing an image of him, and "The Vice Chairman should be healthy forever" at a photo of Lin Biao, Mao's anointed successor. Widely recounted was a story about a peasant who needed money and sold his only pig for a low price. When the buyer suggested that perhaps the animal was ill, the peasant replied defensively, "the pig will be healthy forever." For that, which was taken as an oblique criticism of Lin Biao, the peasant was sentenced to 15 years' hard labor.

This reverence towards Lin Biao ended in 1971, however, when Lin allegedly betrayed the Chairman and died in an air crash over Mongolia. Subsequently, the sentence against the peasant in the story was commuted and he was released and even praised.

回锅肉

Twice-Cooked Pork

Ingredients

1 lb. (450 g.) pork shoulder
3-4 cloves of garlic
2-3 scallions (spring onions)
2 Tbsp. (30 ml.) cooking oil
1 Tbsp. (12 g.) sugar

2 Tbsp. (30 ml.) soy sauce
1 Tbsp. (15 ml.) wine vinegar
1 small chili pepper (½ tsp., or 2.5 ml., of chili oil)

This dish permitted the peasants to make two meals out of one piece of pork. The pork was boiled the first time around to make soup. The next day, it was "returned to the pot" – the actual meaning of the dish's Chinese name – for braising, and became a second course.

Boil enough water to cover the whole piece of pork in a pot and place the pork in it. Turn the heat down to medium, cover the pot tightly and allow to cook for 45 minutes.

Slice the garlic and cut the scallion into ½ inch (1.5 cm.) pieces. When the pork is finished cooking, remove it from the bowl and allow it to cool. You may even refrigerate it for half an hour to an hour. Then cut it into 1/8 inch (3 mm.) thick slices.

Heat the wok and add the cooking oil. When it begins to smoke, fry the garlic and scallions until they emit an aroma. Add the pork, sugar, soy sauce, vinegar and chili pepper (or chili oil) and stir-fry for two minutes. Remove and serve.

Slaughtering Swine with Two Knives

"Hold Chairman Mao's flag high, and follow Chairman Hua to victory," 1977.

When Hua Guofeng was Party Secretary of Hunan Province, he pioneered the "two knives" policy. Peasants wielded the "collective knife" on pigs sold to the state, but were permitted a "private" knife for pigs they raised to feed themselves. The result was that it was not necessary to ration pork in Hunan until 1975, the year he left to join the central government.

Hua became Acting Premier of China on the death of Zhou Enlai and Chairman of the Party upon Mao's demise several months later. Shortly before his death, Mao supposedly wrote to Hua, "with you in charge, my heart is at ease." It was Hua who officially ended the Cultural Revolution after the Gang of Four was arrested in 1976.

雪豆肉片

Sliced Pork with Snow Peas

Ingredients

½ lb. (225 g.) lean pork
1 Tbsp. (15 g.) cornstarch
½ tsp. (2 g.) sugar
2 Tbsp. (30 ml.) soy sauce
½ lb. (225 g.) snow peas

1 scallion (spring onion)
2 cloves garlic
5 Tbsp. (75 ml.) cooking oil
Dash of salt

Like many other dishes in the Chinese repertoire, this consists of meat cooked together with a vegetable. You can substitute many things for the snow peas – a few ideas are celery, bamboo shoots, cabbage and mushrooms. You can also use beef or chicken instead of pork.

Cut the pork into thin slices no more than 1½ inches (4 cm.) long and about ¼ inch (6 mm.) thick. In a bowl, marinate the meat with the cornstarch, sugar and soy sauce. Remove the threads from the snow peas and set aside.

Slice the scallion into pieces about an inch (2.5 cm.) long, and then cut each piece lengthwise into two pieces. Crush the garlic.

Heat the wok until it is very hot and add the oil. When it begins to smoke, stir-fry the garlic for about 10 seconds and then add the scallion and fry for another 10 seconds. When you can smell the aroma of the scallion and garlic, add the pork and stir-fry for about a minute and a half.

Add the snow peas and the salt and continue to fry for another 2-3 minutes until the pork has changed color. Remove and serve.

Cooking for the Hogs

"Grow aquatic plants to develop hog farming," 1973.

Grain was too valuable, and in too short supply, to be wasted on barnyard animals, so peasants actually prepared food for their pigs during the Cultural Revolution.

Since the animals would not naturally graze on grass and grain hulls, these items had to be made palatable by cooking them. Most peasant households had large burners and woks big enough for a person to sit in that were used for this purpose. The grasses were boiled in water that had previously been used to wash rice so that they retained some minimal nutritious value.

青紅椒肉丝

Pork with Green and Red Pepper Shreds

Ingredients

½ lb. (225 g.) lean pork
3 Tbsp. (45 ml.) soy sauce
½ Tbsp. (12 g.) sugar
1 Tbsp. (15 g.) cornstarch

1 large red pepper
1 large green pepper
3-4 cloves garlic
5 Tbsp. (75 ml.) cooking oil

Most stir-fried Chinese dishes are comprised of ingredients of more or less the same size and shape. In this dish, the meat is cut into strips, and the peppers are cut to match. Two different types of peppers are used to give the dish color.

Slice the pork into strips no more than ¼ inch (6 mm.) thick and between 1½ and 2 inches (4-5 cm.) long. Marinate the pork in 2 tablespoons (30 ml.) of the soy sauce plus the sugar and the cornstarch mixed together.

Core the peppers, removing all membranes, and slice them into strips the same size as the pork strips. Crush the garlic.

Heat the wok until it is very hot but don't add any oil. Stir-fry the pepper shreds for approximately five minutes until they soften. When their skin begins to blister, remove them from the wok.

Add the oil to the hot wok. When it begins to smoke, fry the garlic for 30 seconds. Then add the pork and stir-fry it together with the rest of the soy sauce for 2-3 minutes until the meat changes color and is cooked through. Add the peppers and stir-fry the mixture for two minutes. Remove and serve.

Raising "Loyalty Pigs"

"Our production team's great hog keeper,"
1964.

When the Cultural Revolution reached its zenith, "loyalty" was its watchword. People danced a "loyalty dance" and wrote the word everywhere to express devotion to Chairman Mao. In one commune, the peasants found a novel way to express fidelity: they shaved the character for "loyalty" on the heads of the best pigs. Before anyone slaughtered a "loyalty pig," it was the custom to proclaim his or her devotion to the Chairman.

Beef and Lamb

牛羊肉类

"The grasslands are bathed in sunlight," 1972.

红焖牛肉

Braised Beef in Soy Sauce

Ingredients

1½ lbs. (about 700 g.) beef short ribs (boneless beef may also be used, but avoid too tender a cut)
1 small (or ½ large) onion
1 large piece ginger (1 inch, or 2.5 cm., on a side)
2-3 Tbsp. (30-45 ml.) cooking oil
5 Tbsp. (75 ml.) soy sauce
2 Tbsp. (12 g.) sugar
½ cup (120 ml.) wine
2-3 pieces star anise

In old China, cows were not slaughtered until they had outlived their usefulness as beasts of burden, so this dish was traditionally made with aged beef, which was tough and lean – hence its rather lengthy cooking time.

Cut the beef into pieces about two inches (5 cm.) long and an inch (2.5 cm.) wide. If you are using ribs, hack right through the bone so each piece contains a piece of the bone.

Dice the onion into half-inch (about 1.5 cm.) cubes. Crush the ginger.

Heat a wok and add the cooking oil. When it begins to smoke, add the onion and stir-fry until the pieces begin to brown. Then add the ginger, soy sauce and sugar and continue to cook until the mixture begins to bubble.

Add the beef and stir-fry until all the ingredients are well-mixed. Then add the wine and the star anise. Cover the wok and turn the heat down to medium.

Braise for one half hour to 45 minutes, until the beef is falling off the bone (or, if boneless beef is used, until it is very tender). Remove and serve.

Cow Devils and Snake Spirits

"Spring brings the warm weather and the calves gain weight," 1963.

A Chinese tradition holds that those who are hell-bound are escorted there by a cow-devil, and Mao borrowed this term, which is often paired with "snake spirit," to describe enemies of the people. The makeshift jails into which these persecuted people were imprisoned at the hands of the Red Guards and others were thus referred to as "cow sheds." They were fearsome places in which people were often treated quite brutally.

滑蛋牛肉

Fried Beef with Scrambled Eggs

Ingredients

¼ lb. (115 g.) beef flank steak
 (veal may be substituted)
1 Tbsp. (15 ml.) soy sauce (light
 variety if available)
2 Tbsp. (30 g.) cornstarch

½ cup (120 ml.) cold water
3 eggs
Dash of salt
5 Tbsp. (75 ml.) cooking oil

No one would have slaughtered a young calf during the Cultural Revolution, but this dish is actually far tastier if veal is substituted for beef. You can use beef, too, of course. The key is not to overcook the meat.

Slice the meat into pieces about one inch (2.5 cm.) square and ¼ inch (6 mm.) thick. Marinate it in soy sauce and ½ Tbsp. (8 g.) of the cornstarch. Then, in a separate bowl, add the rest of the cornstarch to the water and mix until it dissolves completely and forms a paste. Make sure no lumps remain.

Beat the eggs and add them to the cornstarch mixture. Add the salt. (*Note: the volume of the eggs should be about twice the volume of the water. If it is less, add a fourth egg. If it is more, add some water.*)

Heat the oil in a wok. Before it begins to smoke, stir-fry the beef in it for 15-20 seconds. Remove the beef; it should not yet be fully cooked.

Heat the remaining oil in the wok until it smokes. Pour in the egg mixture and stir-fry. When the eggs begin to solidify, add the beef and stir-fry for another 10-15 seconds, which should permit the beef to finish cooking. Remove from the wok and serve.

Veal at Every Meal

Deng Xiaoping trying on a ten-gallon hat during his 1979 visit to Texas.

Deng Xiaoping loved beef and was especially fond of veal. When he visited the United States in 1979 – the first visit to America by a leader of the People's Republic of China – word of his food preferences preceded him. His American hosts, eager to please, apparently prepared veal for him at almost every opportunity.

When asked by his aides after he returned to China for his dominant impression of the United States, Deng is said to have complained, "Veal, veal, veal at every meal."

卤牛肉

Stewed Beef with Star Anise

Ingredients

2 dried chili peppers
3 pieces star anise
1 small piece ginger (about ½ inch, or 1.5 cm., on a side)
3 whole brown peppercorns
½ stick cinnamon
4-5 whole cloves
2 scallions (spring onions), or one small onion
1 cup (250 ml.) soy sauce (dark is best)
½ cup (120 ml.) wine, any variety
1½ Tbsp. (12 g.) sugar
1 lb. (450 g.) beef shoulder (or any tender, well-marbled cut)

This recipe is similar to the one for Stewed Duck Chaozhou Style that appears on page 61, and the broth from that dish may be used to cook the beef in this recipe. The tendency of the beef to absorb the duck fat will make this dish even tastier.

Combine all the ingredients with the exception of the beef and, in a large stock pot, bring them to a boil in enough water to cover the meat. Lower the heat, cover and let simmer for one hour.

Turn the heat up to high and boil again. Then add the beef and bring back to a boil.

Cover the pot and turn the heat down to medium. Cook for another 15 minutes. Remove the beef and cut it into slices between 1/8" and ¼" (3-6 mm.) thick. Arrange on a platter and serve.

Barefoot Doctors and Veterinarians

"Patriotic production increases on the grasslands. The Inner Mongolian government rewards model workers with well-bred cows," 1952.

Sending urban youth to the countryside made for strange bedfellows. The young people were surprised at how backward the peasants were, and the peasants saw them as highly educated. Peasants chose the urban youth to minister to sick people and animals, and these young people became so-called "barefoot doctors" and "barefoot veterinarians," even though few had had any medical education.

Years later, when schools re-opened in China, many actually entered medical school. Some of China's most prominent physicians got their start as barefoot doctors.

葱爆羊肉

Sliced Lamb with Scallions

Ingredients

6-8 scallions (spring onions)
½ lb., (225 g.) boneless lamb
2 Tbsp. (30 ml.) soy sauce
2-3 Tbsp. (30-45 ml.) wine (any variety)

1 Tbsp. (15 g.) cornstarch
1 tsp. (4 g.) sugar
5 Tbsp. (75 ml.) cooking oil
2 slices ginger (each about the size of a quarter or a 2p coin)

This is a Mongolian dish, also favored by Chinese Muslims, made with a northern Chinese variety of scallions that are mostly white with very little green at the ends, and are sweeter than the American variety. But feel free to use American scallions or, for a variation, one large leek, cut into thin pieces.

Slice the scallions into two-inch lengths. Slice the lamb into matchsticks, each about 1½ inches (4 cm.) long and 1/8 inch (3 mm.) thick. Marinate the lamb in a mixture of the soy sauce, wine, cornstarch and sugar.

Heat a wok until it is very hot and then pour in the oil, which should begin to smoke very quickly. Add the ginger and scallions and stir-fry for just a few seconds. Then add the lamb and continue to stir-fry for about a half a minute. Remove and serve.

Little Heroines of the Grasslands

Long Mei and Yu Rong, two sisters from Inner Mongolia aged 12 and 9, respectively, were assigned the duty of herding their commune's sheep in 1964. A sudden snowstorm scattered the sheep, however, and rather than return home, they followed the herd and attempted to catch stray lambs. The next day, when the two girls were found, they were 20 miles from home and had collapsed of exposure. When they were revived, they wanted only to know whether the lambs were safe. They had lost only three of the 384 sheep, and were praised in the national media as examples for young people all over China.

羊肉炖红萝卜

Stewed Lamb Shank with Carrots

Ingredients

1 lamb shank
1 medium-sized piece ginger
(about ½ inch, or 1.5 cm., on a side)
3 large carrots
1 Tbsp. (15 ml.) cooking oil
½ stick cinnamon (optional)

½ tsp. (1.5 g.) dried dill weed
(optional)
Zest of ¼ of an orange (optional)
4 Tbsp. (60 ml.) soy sauce
2 Tbsp. (25 g.) sugar
1 cup (250 ml.) wine

Carrots are wonderful in this dish, because they absorb the lamb's flavor. But broccoli, cauliflower and potatoes, steamed or boiled and added 2-3 minutes before the dish is done, also work well.

Put enough water to cover the lamb shank in a large pot over high heat and bring to a boil. Add the lamb and return to a boil. Simmer for five minutes over medium heat and remove the lamb. Crush the ginger and cut the carrots on the bias into two-inch (5 cm.) lengths.

Heat a wok over a medium flame and add the oil. Then add the ginger and any or all of the three optional ingredients. Turn the heat down to low and stir-fry until you can smell the fragrance.

Add the lamb shank, soy sauce, sugar and wine and cover tightly. Cook over low heat for about 30 minutes. Add the carrots, re-cover and cook for an additional 10 minutes. The dish is done when the lamb is nearly falling off the bone.

A Grasslands Lament

"The animal husbandry cooperative helps its ewes give birth," 1956.

Even the songs people were permitted to sing were limited during the Cultural Revolution. The sad songs of the "sent-down youth" about the difficulty of life on the farms were not revolutionary and were forbidden, but this did not stop the youngsters from writing and singing them.

One student sent to Inner Mongolia sang of his lonely life as a shepherd:

"The sheep eat the grass, and the scene is so peaceful
I stand and look around me
Another herd of sheep is far away
I stand alone and wish I could talk with them
And my heart feels so sad."

Seafood

海鲜类

"The commune's fish pond," 1973.

姜葱油淋鱼

Dredged Fish with Ginger and Scallions

Ingredients

½ lb. (225 g.) any white meat, salt water fish (*e.g.*, cod, sea bass, halibut) cut into one-inch (2.5 cm.) thick slices

½ cup (75 g.) bread crumbs

6-7 Tbsp. (about 100 ml.) cooking

oil

1 medium-sized piece ginger (about ½ inch, or 1.5 cm., on a side)

1 scallion (spring onion)

2-3 Tbsp. (30-45 ml.) soy sauce

Ginger and scallions work in beautiful harmony together, but if they are overcooked they lose flavor. In this dish they are barely cooked at all. The hot oil takes the edge off of them, and they retain a delightful, fresh taste.

Dredge the fish slices in the bread crumbs so they are lightly coated on both sides. Then heat 2-3 Tbsp. (30-45 ml.) of the oil in a wok until it begins to smoke. Place the fish slices in the wok and allow them to brown on one side – this should take about one and a half to two minutes. Then turn them and brown the other side. Try to turn them only once so they don't fall apart.

Slice the ginger and scallion into slender matchsticks, about an inch (2.5 cm.) long and 1/8 inch (6 mm.) thick. Remove the fish slices from the wok and place them on a serving plate. Then add the rest of the oil to the wok and heat it until it begins to smoke.

Sprinkle the pieces of raw scallion and ginger on the fish and then pour the hot cooking oil on top of it. The oil will cook the raw ingredients outside of the wok. Finally, drizzle the soy sauce on top and serve.

Big Character Posters

Posting "big character posters" on walls was a key method of expressing oneself during the Cultural Revolution. People used them to show their agreement with Party policies and to criticize their enemies. Almost from the beginning, children of the Party's targets were encouraged to denounce their parents, and this was often done publicly through posters.

When He Long, a communist military hero in Beijing, came under attack, his daughter wrote a "big character poster" accusing him of counterrevolutionary activities, among which were his bourgeois habit of going fishing and his delight in eating seafood. He's persecution ended with his death in 1969 at the age of 73.

香煎三文鱼

Pan-Fried Salmon in a Fragrant Sauce

Ingredients

2 scallions (spring onions)
3-4 Tbsp. (45-60 ml.) cooking oil
1 large salmon filet (about ½ inch

to an inch, or 1.5-2.5 cm., thick)
2 Tbsp. (30 ml.) soy sauce (light
variety preferred)

In this dish, the salmon spends only about 20 seconds over a flame. Most of the cooking comes from the hot oil in which it sits. Overcooking is the worst crime you could commit in preparing this dish – less is more here.

Slice the scallions on the bias into two-inch (5 cm.) lengths. Then heat the oil in a flat-bottomed pan until it begins to smoke. Add the salmon and pan-fry it on one side for about 10 seconds, or a little longer if it is a thicker filet. Then quickly turn it over and add the scallions.

After another 10 seconds, cover the pan tightly and turn off the heat. Allow the pan to sit on the burner for one additional minute.

Remove from the wok, sprinkle with the soy sauce, and serve.

War Over Salmon

"With hatred in one's breast, one will never miss the target," ca. 1970.

Few Chinese had ever seen salmon in 1969 – it is native only to northeast China. But that did not stop the country from fighting for the fish. In a border skirmish with the Soviets over an island in the Ussuri River, Chinese fighters clashed with Russian troops to demonstrate that China would not be bullied. The Party built support for the action by stressing, in propaganda, the strategic importance of the region: wonderful salmon.

姜葱焗蟹

Crab with Ginger and Scallions

Ingredients

4 small or medium-sized blue
    crabs
3-4 scallions (spring onions)
1 large piece ginger (about 1 inch,
    or 2.5 cm., on a side)

3-4 Tbsp. (45-60 ml.) cooking oil
1 Tbsp. (15 ml.) rice wine (but any
    other wine will do)
2 eggs

The most unpleasant aspect of this recipe is cleaning the crabs. If you're not up to the task, have the fishmonger do it for you. Just don't plan on cooking first and cleaning after – it will ruin the taste.

Clean the crabs, removing inedible parts such as the gills, which are the spongy white tissue under the shell, and the eyes. Rinse thoroughly. If the crabs are medium-sized, use a cleaver to crack the shells and hack them into smaller pieces. If you are using small crabs, you can work with them whole.

Cut the scallions into one-inch (2.5 cm.) lengths and smash the ginger with the side of the cleaver. Heat a wok and add the oil to it. When the oil begins to smoke, add the ginger, and a few second later – after you can smell the aroma of the ginger – add the scallions. When you can smell the ginger and scallion mix, add the crab and the wine. Cover the wok tightly and cook for seven minutes.

Beat the eggs, add them to the wok and stir. In about 10-15 seconds, after the eggs have cooked and the sauce has thickened, remove everything from the wok and serve.

Three He-Crabs, One She-Crab

"The Gang of Four Shows Their True Colors,"
1977.

When the leftist "Gang of Four" – which had persecuted thousands and which included Mao's wife Jiang Qing – was purged in 1976, no one dared celebrate openly until the rumors were confirmed. Beijing's crab sellers jumped the gun, however, hitting the streets with a special, symbolic deal on three males and one female crab. Because "walking sideways" is a Chinese term for disregarding the rights and feelings of others, crabs were a particularly appropriate symbol for the hated quartet.

大虾青菜

Prawns with Cooked Greens

Ingredients

1 lb. (450 g.) leafy green vegetable (kale, collard greens, mustard greens, broccoli rabe or brussels sprouts all work well)

2 Tbsp. (30 ml.) cooking oil

10 large prawns, peeled and deveined

2 Tbsp. (30 ml.) oyster sauce (or, if unavailable, soy sauce)

¼ tsp. (1 g.) sugar

¼ tsp. pepper

½ Tbsp. (8 ml.) sesame oil

Color is important in Chinese cooking. In this dish, the greens and the shrimp are not cooked together, but they are served together because the green and red colors complement each other so well.

Heat the water in a pot or a wok and boil or steam the green vegetable until it is cooked through. Remove and put aside. Then heat the oil in a wok until it begins to smoke.

Add the prawns and stir-fry them until they change color. Then add the oyster sauce (or soy sauce) and sugar. Continue to stir-fry for 15 seconds and then remove everything from the wok.

Arrange the green vegetable on a platter and place the prawns on top. Sprinkle with the pepper and drizzle the sesame oil on top and serve.

The Importance of Overseas Relatives

A five-yuan Overseas Chinese voucher from Guangxi Autonomous Region.

Depending on where you lived, shrimp was either easily available in local streams or nearly impossible to get during the Cultural Revolution. Lucky city dwellers with relatives in Hong Kong or overseas could receive remittances from them in the form of "Overseas Chinese Foreign Currency" certificates. These could be used, with cash, at special state-run stores that stocked hard-to-find foodstuffs like prawns, meat, beans and cooking oil as well as cloth and other household goods.

腰果虾仁

Stir-Fried Shrimp with Cashew Nuts

Ingredients

1 lb. (450 g.) shrimp, peeled and deveined
1 Tbsp. (15 g.) cornstarch
1 egg white
2 tsp. (10 ml.) soy sauce
½ tsp. (2 g.) sugar
3 slices ginger (each the size of a quarter or a 2p coin)
1 scallion (spring onion)
2-3 Tbsp. (30-45 ml.) cooking oil
Dash of salt (optional)
½ cup (60 g.) roasted cashew nuts (salted or unsalted)

Peanuts and walnuts are acceptable substitutes, but this dish is customarily made with cashews, which themselves have a shrimp-like shape.

Prepare the shrimp, if necessary, by peeling and then slicing through the back and removing the vein. Slice most, but not all, of the way through. Using the side of a cleaver, pat the shrimp lightly to flatten it. Mix the cornstarch, egg white, soy sauce and sugar and use the mixture as a marinade for the shrimp. Crush the ginger and slice the scallion into small pieces, about an inch (2.5 cm.) long.

Heat the wok and add the cooking oil. When the oil is very hot, add the ginger and scallions and stir-fry them quickly for 10-15 seconds. Then add the shrimp and cook for another minute and a half. Add the salt if you are using unsalted cashews. When the shrimp turns red and curls up, turn off the heat. Add the cashew nuts and mix them in until they are warm. Remove and serve.

Note: Chinese peasant cooks would have felt that using egg white in a marinade was a waste of a good egg, but it really improves the texture of the dish.

Farming the Borderlands

Veteran soldiers working on a military farm.

Cashew nuts, native to Brazil, were introduced in China in 1958. Tropical plants, they were farmed on Hainan Island, just off the coast of south China, by retired soldiers in what were called production and construction military camps.

These huge farms had several purposes: they served as a jobs and a settlement program for retired soldiers, and were a way to build up border areas and shore up China's defenses at the same time. As the old soldiers died off, the farms needed laborers, and they absorbed hundreds of thousands of the young, urban "sent-down youth" whom Mao dispatched to the countryside in 1968.

青红椒虾仁

Shrimp with Green and Red Peppers

Ingredients

1 lb. (450 g.) small or medium-sized shrimp, peeled and deveined

½ tsp. (2.5 ml.) vinegar (any variety)

1 Tbsp. (12 g.) sugar

2 Tbsp. (30 ml.) soy sauce (light variety if available)

1 Tbsp. (15 g.) cornstarch

1½ green and/or red bell peppers

2-3 cloves garlic

4 Tbsp. (60 ml.) cooking oil

The peppers are cooked without oil in this dish to rid them of any bitter taste. You can substitute sweet red peppers or any variety of hot pepper, but if you use yellow bell peppers, which have no bitter taste, you may use oil.

Marinate the shrimp in a mixture of the vinegar, sugar, soy sauce and cornstarch. Slice the peppers into pieces about two inches (5 cm.) long and ¼ inch (6 mm.) wide.

Crush the garlic. Heat a wok – without any oil – and stir-fry the pepper pieces briefly until they soften. Leave them in the wok for 2-3 minutes, but remove before they turn color.

Heat the wok again, still without any oil. When it is very hot, add the oil. Once it begins to smoke, which will be within a few seconds, add the garlic and stir-fry for 10 seconds. Then add the shrimp and stir-fry until it turns color and cooks through – about a minute and a half.

Add the pepper and mix well. Remove and serve.

Don't Learn Painting from Qi Baishi

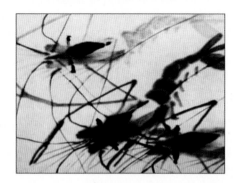

Qi Baishi, arguably China's most famous 20th century artist, was known internationally for his stylized paintings of shrimp. Although he died in 1957, he was nonetheless severely denounced by the Red Guards years later, mainly because of Chairman Mao's ludicrous condemnation of him.

Mao excoriated Qi and another painter because they never painted the human form, and concluded that they did not do so because they did not know how. Mao, like many socialists, appreciated realism and had little use for abstraction. He felt that revolutionary students of painting should paint reality and not waste their time learning from the likes of Qi Baishi.

葱烧鱼

Braised Fish with Scallions

Ingredients

1 large piece ginger (about 1 inch, or 2.5 cm., on a side)
2-3 cloves garlic
15 scallions (spring onions)
5-6 Tbsp. (75-90 ml.) cooking oil
1 whole fresh water fish (*e.g.,* tilapia, pike or perch), about 1-1½ lbs. (450-700 g.)
2 Tbsp. (30 ml.) white vinegar
1 Tbsp. (12 g.) sugar
4 Tbsp. (60 ml.) soy sauce

The Chinese take pride in keeping fish whole in dishes like this – they don't like to see heads or fins cut off. If you feel differently, you can use filets. But be sure to use fresh-water fish – it tastes better in this dish than salt-water fish.

Smash the ginger and the garlic with the side of a cleaver and cut each of the scallions into two pieces, separating the thick, white portion from the thinner green portion. Heat a wok until it is very hot, and then add the oil. Before the oil begins to smoke, add the ginger.

When you can smell the aroma of the ginger, add the fish to the wok. Turn the heat down to medium and fry each side for 2-3 minutes until the skin begins to brown. Then add the vinegar and sugar, making sure the sugar dissolves, and add the soy sauce. When the mixture begins to boil, add the thick pieces of scallion, cook briefly, and then add the thin pieces. Then cover the wok and turn the heat down a bit more.

Cook for 10 minutes. Remove the fish, taking care to keep it in one piece if possible. Cover with the other ingredients and serve.

Little Red Guards and a Carp

"Abundant grain and fish – a double harvest."

A popular story told of two "Little Red Guards" who were taking care of a pregnant sow for their production team. The boys caught a carp just as the pig bore several piglets. Since carp is considered especially good for nursing women, the boys cooked the fish and fed it to the sow instead of eating it themselves. When they learned later that the fish had escaped from a neighboring collective, these model socialist children raised money and repaid the original owners for its loss.

清蒸全鱼

Steamed Whole Fish

Ingredients

1 whole fish (about 1-1½ lbs.) or 2 whole fish (about ½ lb. each) cleaned and scaled, head and tail on (snapper, flounder, pike, bass and tilapia all work well)

3 cups cold water

1 large piece ginger (about 1 inch on a side)

2 scallions

2-3 Tbsp. cooking oil

2-3 Tbsp. soy sauce

This dish tastes equally good with fresh water or salt-water fish, as long as the fish is very fresh. Check the eyes – clear means fresh; murky means look elsewhere. In this dish, you can't get away with two-day old fish.

If the fish is an inch (2.5 cm.) thick or thicker, score its sides widthwise, making cuts every inch and a half (3-4 cm.) and slicing nearly to the bone to facilitate cooking. If the fish is thinner than that, this step may be omitted.

Bring the water to a boil in a wok or a steamer. Cut the ginger and scallions into shreds about an inch and a half (4 cm.) in length and as thin as you can make them.

Arrange the fish on a platter and cover with half the ginger. Then suspend the plate over the boiling water, making sure it is not submerged, and cover the wok or steamer tightly. Steam for 8-10 minutes until the eyeballs pop out.

Remove and drain any excess water from the plate. Heat the oil in a microwave for 15 seconds. Sprinkle the scallions and the rest of the ginger and drizzle the oil and the soy sauce on top and serve.

The People's Liberation Army is Like Fish

"The people are like water and the army is like fish," Mao Zedong wrote in 1948 as a tribute to guerilla warfare, and the quote was recycled whenever he needed to mobilize the military, sometimes to solve problems of his own making. The refrain was commonly heard in the mid-1960s before the Cultural Revolution and was used in 1968 when Mao commanded the People's Liberation Army to send the marauding students off to the countryside. Most people, tired of the chaos, were relieved to see order restored, but it was a mixed bag, because the military's brand of order could be a brutal one.

Eggs
鸡蛋类

"Healthy chickens lay large eggs," 1964.

茶叶蛋

Marbled Eggs Steeped in Tea

Ingredients

1 dozen eggs (more or fewer, depending on the number being served)

1 stick cinnamon

2 tsp. (10 ml.) soy sauce

1 tsp. (6 g.) salt

2 tea bags (any variety but herbal tea)

The Chinese don't just drink tea – they also sometimes cook with it. But during the Cultural Revolution, no self-respecting peasant would have cooked eggs with fresh tea leaves, only used leaves would do. Steeping eggs in tea gives them a remarkably pleasant flavor – as well as a beautiful marbling pattern.

Make sure eggs are at room temperature before you begin. Hard-boil the eggs in water for 10 minutes. Remove the eggs from the pot, but reserve the water. After the eggs have cooled, tap on the eggshells with a metal spoon until they crack all over. Since the cracking will be responsible for the marbling later, make sure there are several cracks that penetrate the shell in each egg.

Add all the other ingredients to the hot water and put the cracked eggs back in. At very low heat, steep the eggs for 45 minutes. Then turn off the heat and let the eggs soak up to 24 hours; longer is better.

Remove the shells to reveal the marbled eggs. Sprinkle with additional salt before serving, if desired.

Saving "Big Red Robe" Tea

"Young girls picking tea leaves," 1964.

Red Guards came through the town of Wuyishan in Fujian Province in 1966 and set out to cut down the bushes from which a local production brigade produced Dahongpao tea. The brand name – which meant "big red robe" – had feudalistic connotations, since men who passed the civil service exams in imperial China had traditionally been honored with red robes.

It took an expert from the local government tea institute to save the tea. He pointed out that the tea was a favorite of Chairman Mao and Marshall Zhu De. And if revolutionaries like them liked it, wasn't it by definition "revolutionary"? Rather than risk being "class enemies" themselves, the guards departed, and the tea was saved – but it was renamed Dahongmei – "big red plum" tea.

清蒸蛋羹

Steamed Savory Egg Custard

Ingredients

2 eggs
3½ cups (900 ml.) cold water
Dash of salt
¼ scallion (spring onion)

½ Tbsp. (8 ml.) sesame oil
(optional)
Sprig of cilantro or parsley (for
garnish; optional)

This was a particularly popular dish during the Cultural Revolution because it did not require oil, which was strictly rationed, and because portions could be increased by dilution so that adding more water meant feeding more people.

Beat the eggs in a dish and add one and a half cups (about 400 ml.) of the water and the salt. Mix well. Cut the scallion into small pieces.

Put the mixture in a heat-safe dish with a cover. The covered dish should fit inside your wok. Add the remaining water to the wok and bring to a boil.

When the water begins to boil, place the covered dish in the wok and then cover the wok itself. Turn the heat down to medium and simmer for 10 minutes.

Remove from the wok. Just before serving, sprinkle the scallion and drizzle the sesame oil (if desired) on top of the custard. Garnish and serve.

The Chicken Butt Bank

Despite periodic crackdowns during the Cultural Revolution, many peasants surreptitiously kept chickens in their yards as a source of eggs. Once past their egg-laying prime, the chickens, too, were eaten.

Eggs could be sold in local markets and were a major source of a meager cash income. This gave rise to what many referred to jokingly as the "chicken butt bank." During extended crackdowns such as the fever-pitched early 1970s, a chicken in your yard could earn you public humiliation and even a "struggle session," in which you could be dragged up on stage in front of a large crowd and denounced.

番茄炒蛋

Scrambled Eggs with Tomatoes

Ingredients

2 large or 4 small tomatoes
4 eggs
5 Tbsp. (75 ml.) vegetable oil
4 Tbsp. (50 g.) sugar

Dash of salt
Several sprigs of cilantro or
    parsley (for garnish; optional)

This is a very common dish in north China, where the tomatoes tend to be sweeter and less watery than the southern variety. Tomatoes and eggs may sound like strange bedfellows, but they complement each other remarkably well in this dish.

Cut the tomatoes into wedges, each no more than an inch (2.5 cm.) thick at its widest point. Squeeze out the excess liquid in each, but reserve the liquid. It is not necessary to remove all of the seeds.

Break the eggs in a bowl, add the liquid from the tomatoes, and beat the mixture together.

Put the oil in a wok and heat it until it begins to smoke. Stir-fry the egg mixture quickly until it solidifies – this should take about a minute. Remove from the wok.

Stir-fry the tomatoes for 4-5 minutes until they lose their resilience. Then add the sugar and continue to stir-fry until it dissolves. Allow to boil for a full minute and then add the egg mixture.

Stir-fry for less than a minute until the eggs are thoroughly cooked. Remove from the wok and add the salt. Garnish with cilantro or parsley, if desired.

Enough Geometry for the Chairman

"An armband worn by a member of the Beijing Capital Red Guard Army," ca. 1966.

In July 1968, a few months before Mao decided to dispatch China's urban youth to the countryside, he met with a group of Red Guard leaders and told them formal education was overrated.

"I never followed the rules when I was in school; my bottom line was just not to get expelled," he declared. "For my exams, anything over 50-60 was fine; so was anything under 80; 70 was my baseline. I didn't care about many subjects, though sometimes I had to study them. Occasionally, I would just hand in a blank sheet of paper. In geometry, I just drew a picture of an egg – that was enough geometry for me."

摊黄菜

Savory Golden Omelet

Ingredients

3 eggs
½ cup (120 ml.) cold water
1 Tbsp. (15 g.) cornstarch

¼ tsp. (2 g.) salt
5 Tbsp. (75 ml.) cooking oil

*In the countryside, this dish is often made with animal fat –
usually duck or pork fat. But the healthier variety uses vegetable
oil, and still tastes decidedly better than plain fried eggs.*

Beat the eggs and mix them with the water, cornstarch
and salt. Then heat a flat-bottomed pan until it is
extremely hot. Add the oil, which should begin to
smoke almost immediately.

After the oil smokes, add the egg mixture and make sure
it coats the bottom of the pan, but keep it about a half-inch
(1.5 cm.) thick.

When it begins to form a crust on the bottom, turn off the
heat and flip the omelet over. Let it sit for a minute; it should
be crusty on the outside but soft in the middle. Remove and
serve.

Finding a Bone Inside an Egg

*Denunciation of Heilongjiang Provincial
Party Secretary Ren Zhongyi, 1966.*

Five classes of people – former landlords,
rich peasants, counterrevolutionaries,
rightists and "bad elements" – were sin-
gled out as targets during the Cultural
Revolution, but anyone could be the
subject of persecution. Popular methods
of humiliating victims included parad-
ing them around the streets in a dunce
cap and forcing them onto a stage to be
denounced by the audience. If there was
nothing specific to criticize about an in-
nocent target, charges might be fabricated.
This was known as "finding a bone inside
an egg."

韭菜炒鸡蛋

Fried Eggs with Chives

Ingredients

1 large bunch chives (about the diameter of a half dollar, or 30 mm.)

4 eggs
Dash of salt
5 Tbsp. (75 ml.) cooking oil

The Chinese adore this combination of flavors; they feel eggs and chives are a match made in heaven. This dish was popular among peasants and sent-down youth, because both principal ingredients could be raised at home legally and consumed privately during most of the Cultural Revolution.

Rinse off the chives and cut them into small pieces, each about an inch (2.5 cm.) in length. Beat the eggs and add the salt. Heat the oil in a wok. When it begins to smoke, add the chives and stir-fry them until their color changes into a deep green. This should take about a minute.

Add the eggs and stir-fry until they solidify. Remove and serve.

The Son of a Reactionary is a Rotten Egg

"Be a person like this one," 1971.

"Rotten egg" is an epithet the Chinese use to describe bad people. In the mid-1960s, when the Red Guards were formed, they welcomed only the "right" kind of people: the sons and daughters of Party officials. One of their slogans justified their selectivity by visiting the sins of the fathers upon the sons: "The son of a hero is a warrior; the son of a reactionary is a rotten egg."

Rice and
Noodles

米饭面条类

"Grain spreads over the ground. The more revolutionary we are, the higher is our grain production," 1965.

虾仁炒饭

Fried Rice with Shrimp

Ingredients

1 cup (150 g.) uncooked rice
3 cups (750 ml.) cold water
1 scallion (spring onion)
2 Tbsp. (30 ml.) cooking oil
1 egg

¼ lb. (115 g.) small or medium
   shrimp, shelled and deveined
2 Tbsp. (30 ml.) soy sauce
Dash of pepper

There are many varieties of rice in China. Long-grain rice works better in this dish because it's less sticky than other varieties. In your supermarket, look for jasmine rice, which is absolutely the best for frying.

Wash and rinse the rice, and then place it in a pot with the water and cover tightly. Bring it to a boil and then immediately turn the flame down to low. In about 10 minutes, the water will all be absorbed and the rice will be ready.

Chop the scallion into small pieces – about ¼ inch (6 mm.) lengths. Then place a wok over high heat and add the cooking oil. When it begins to smoke, crack the egg and add it to the wok. Scramble the egg.

Add the shrimp and the scallion. Stir-fry between a half minute and a minute, depending on the size of the shrimp. Once the shrimp has turned color, stir in the soy sauce and then immediately add the rice. Stir-fry for half a minute. Remove, add pepper, and serve.

Frying Cold Rice

"A scene of rice threshing," 1965.

Chinese cooks use leftover rice for fried rice. "Frying cold rice," however, is also a political term for rehashing. The Cultural Revolution involved so many campaigns that people soon wearied of them. When a new one began, you could more or less recycle activities from past campaigns. Nobody said so out loud, but each time a new order came down, people whispered that it was just another case of "frying cold rice."

鸡丝麻油凉面

Cold Sesame Noodles with Chicken

Ingredients

2 quarts (1.9 liters) cold water
½ boneless chicken breast
¼ lb. (115 g.) spaghetti, linguini
  or similar variety of noodles
2 cloves garlic
5 sprigs cilantro
1 Tbsp. (15 ml.) cooking oil
1 tsp. (2 g.) crushed chili pepper

(or a few drops of chili oil as a
  substitute)
2-3 Tbsp. (30-45 ml.) soy sauce
  (light variety, if available)
1 Tbsp. (15 ml.) vinegar (dark is
  best, but any variety will do)
2 Tbsp. (30 ml.) sesame oil

Sesame oil was hard to get during the Cultural Revolution, and was used sparingly – just a few drops made a big difference.

Boil the water in a pot and add the chicken. Return to a boil and let it sit for 5-7 minutes over medium heat until thoroughly cooked. Remove the chicken and bring the water to a boil a third time, and then add the noodles. When the noodles are fully cooked, remove and drain, and then rinse them in cold water immediately to prevent further cooking and sticking.

Crush the garlic and chop the cilantro roughly. Shred the chicken into matchsticks.

Heat the cooking oil in a wok. Stir-fry the garlic and chili pepper (or chili oil) for 15 seconds. Then turn off the heat. Place the noodles in a bowl and sprinkle with soy sauce and vinegar. Add half of the chili/garlic mix and the sesame oil. Mix well and transfer to a serving plate. Place the chicken shreds on top together with the other half of the chili/garlic mixture. Sprinkle with the cilantro and serve.

Long Life Noodles for the Chairman

Chairman Mao, President Gerald Ford and Henry Kissinger, 1975.

According to Chinese tradition, elderly people celebrate birthdays by eating "long-life noodles." The longer the noodles, the better, and sometimes a whole bowl consisting of one continuous noodle is served up.

In 1975, when Mao turned 82, he celebrated with a few aides, his two daughters and his mistress, Zhang Yufeng. Mao's chefs made noodles by hand for the occasion, but when they started cooking them, the noodles inexplicably all broke into pieces, something that had never happened before. They saved the day by switching to dried noodles. The Chairman couldn't tell the difference, but the chefs saw it as an ill omen. And sure enough, Mao did not live to see another birthday.

肉丝炒面

Stir-Fried Noodles with Pork Shreds

Ingredients

2 quarts (1.9 liters) cold water
¼ lb. (115 g.) spaghetti, linguini
   or similar variety of noodles
¼ lb. (115 g.) lean pork

3 Tbsp. (45 ml.) soy sauce
1 tsp. (6 g.) cornstarch
3-4 scallions (spring onions)
5 Tbsp. (75 ml.) cooking oil

You would have had to look long and hard in China during the Cultural Revolution to find noodles made with eggs, which were always precious. But egg noodles make this dish taste much better than those made with just flour and water. Use dried spaghetti; it's less likely to get soggy than the fresh pasta available in the supermarket.

Bring the water to a boil in a pot and add the noodles. When the noodles are still *al dente*, not soft, remove, drain and rinse in cold water. Then slice the pork into strips about the thickness of a chopstick – ¼ inch (6 mm.) – and about two inches (5 cm.) long.

Marinate the pork in a mixture of 1 Tbsp. (15 ml.) of the soy sauce and the cornstarch, making sure to eliminate any lumps in the cornstarch. Cut the scallion into two-inch (5 cm.) lengths.

Place a wok over a high flame and add the cooking oil. Once the oil is very hot and has been smoking for about 10 seconds, add the meat. Stir-fry for about 10 seconds until the pork changes color and then add the scallion. When the meat is fully cooked – within a minute or so – add the noodles and the rest of the soy sauce and continue to stir-fry for another minute. Remove and serve.

"Sanitary" Noodles

WEI SHENG
Mian Tiao

The Cultural Revolution did not spell the death of brand names in China, but brands and packaging had to fit the political climate, and became more about politics than the products themselves. Producers of foodstuffs and housewares wanted to show they were serving the people, so quotes from Mao were often displayed on packaging. This package of "Sanitary" noodles trumpeted Mao's proclamation that "political work is the lifeline of all economic work." Other brands of the era included "Worker-Peasant" cookies, "The Masses" bread, "Great Leap Forward" shoes, and "East Wind" bicycles.

什锦炒饭

Fried Rice with Ten Delicacies

Ingredients

3 cups (750 ml.) cold water
1 cup (150 g.) uncooked rice
2-3 Tbsp. (30-45 ml.) cooking oil
2 Tbsp. (30 ml.) soy sauce
1 egg
1 scallion (spring onion)
Any eight of the following:
• 1 small carrot
• 2 spears asparagus
• 1 small bamboo shoot (about 1

inch, or 2.5 cm., on a side)
• 2 leaves Napa cabbage
• 5-6 snow pea pods
• 1 stalk celery
• 1 small piece sausage (any
  variety)
• 1 small piece cooked, lean meat
• 3-4 medium shrimp (or 10 small
  shrimp)
• 2-3 white mushrooms

If you're using leftover rice for this dish, as the Chinese do, heat it in the microwave first. This makes it easier to stir-fry than if you try to use it right out of the refrigerator.

Pour the water in a large pot, add the rice and cover. Boil and turn the flame down to low. In 10 minutes, the water should all be absorbed and the rice should be ready.

Chop the other solid ingredients into pieces of about a quarter of an inch (6 mm.) thick. Heat a wok and add the cooking oil. When it begins to smoke, add the egg and scramble it. Add all the other ingredients, in order of thickness and density, since carrots and celery, for example, take longer to cook than scallions. Stir-fry for two minutes until no liquid is visible. Then add the soy sauce and mix well.

Add the cooked rice and stir-fry for 30 seconds. Remove and serve.

The "Iron Rice Bowl"

"Studying and working in the field cultivates crops and people," 1966.

The metaphor in China for one's livelihood is one's "rice bowl," and the guaranteed employment promised by socialism – which managed to turn otherwise industrious people into slackers – was called the "iron rice bowl." The system was highly praised during the Cultural Revolution, and summarily discarded by Mao's successors soon after it was over.

蛋炒饭

Fried Rice with Eggs

Ingredients

1 cup (150 g.) uncooked rice
3 cups (750 ml.) cold water
1 scallion (spring onion)
3 eggs
2 tsp. (10 ml.) cold water

3 Tbsp. (45 ml.) oil
2 Tbsp. (30 ml.) soy sauce
½ small carrot (optional)
3-4 mushrooms (optional)

This very simple dish was a special treat among the peasants and the sent-down youth. Fried rice and eggs was a perfectly appropriate meal to celebrate a child's birthday, a minor holiday or another special occasion.

Rinse off the rice and add it, with the three cups of water, to a pot. Cover tightly and bring to a boil. Then turn the burner down to low and let it sit for another 10 minutes. The rice is ready when the water is completely absorbed.

Let the rice cool for at least a half an hour. In the meantime, slice the scallion into quarter-inch (6 mm.) pieces and the carrot and mushrooms, if desired, into pieces of about the same size. Beat the eggs with the two teaspoons of cold water.

Heat a wok and add the oil. When it begins to smoke, add the eggs and scramble them. Add the scallion and the soy sauce and mix well. Then add the rice. Stir-fry for a minute, remove and serve.

Struggling alongside the Peasants

"Get practice in the real struggle, take root among the workers and peasants and get intellectuals accustomed to manual labor," 1965.

Mao had little use for intellectuals, who suffered greatly during the Cultural Revolution. In the old society, he explained, intellectuals were beholden to imperialists, feudalists and capitalists for their rice – the universal symbol of livelihood among the Chinese. In the new China, intellectuals would derive their sustenance from the proletariat, and to do this, Mao said, they had to "take root" among the workers and peasants and struggle alongside them. Many of those exiled to the countryside continue to believe that they - and China - wasted their most productive years as a result.

捞面

Lo Mein

Ingredients

2 quarts (1.9 liters) cold water
¼ lb. (115 g.) spaghetti, linguini
  or similar variety noodles
Spinach, lettuce, or other green
  vegetable (for garnish)
½ medium (or one small) onion

2 cloves garlic
1 Tbsp. (15 ml.) cooking oil
¼ lb. (115 g.) minced pork (or
  beef)
Dash of sugar
3 Tbsp. (45 ml.) soy sauce

You'll find different varieties of this dish in different parts of China. Its name translates roughly as "drained noodles," and people often place their leftovers on top of it. Feel free to do the same.

Bring the water to a boil in a pot and add the noodles. When they are fully cooked, remove and drain them, and arrange them on a serving platter on top of the spinach, lettuce or green vegetable leaves.

Dice the onion into ½ inch (1.5 cm.) cubes and crush the garlic. Heat the oil in a wok and stir-fry the garlic and onion until the latter turns translucent. Add the minced pork and stir-fry, making sure that the meat does not cling together in clumps.

When no liquid remains in the wok and the meat is fully cooked, add the sugar and soy sauce. Cook for another 30 seconds and then place the mixture on top of the noodles and serve.

Comrade Deng Learns to Make Noodles

Deng Xiaoping was purged for the first time in 1966, a few months after Mao launched the Cultural Revolution. He was sent to work in a factory in Jiangxi Province, while his daughter Deng Rong was sent to a village in faraway Shaanxi. In the early 1970s the family was reunited, and Deng Rong, who had learned the art of making noodles in Shaanxi, taught her father how to do it. According to her memoir, he got good at it and never forgot it even after returning to power in 1973 and again in 1977.

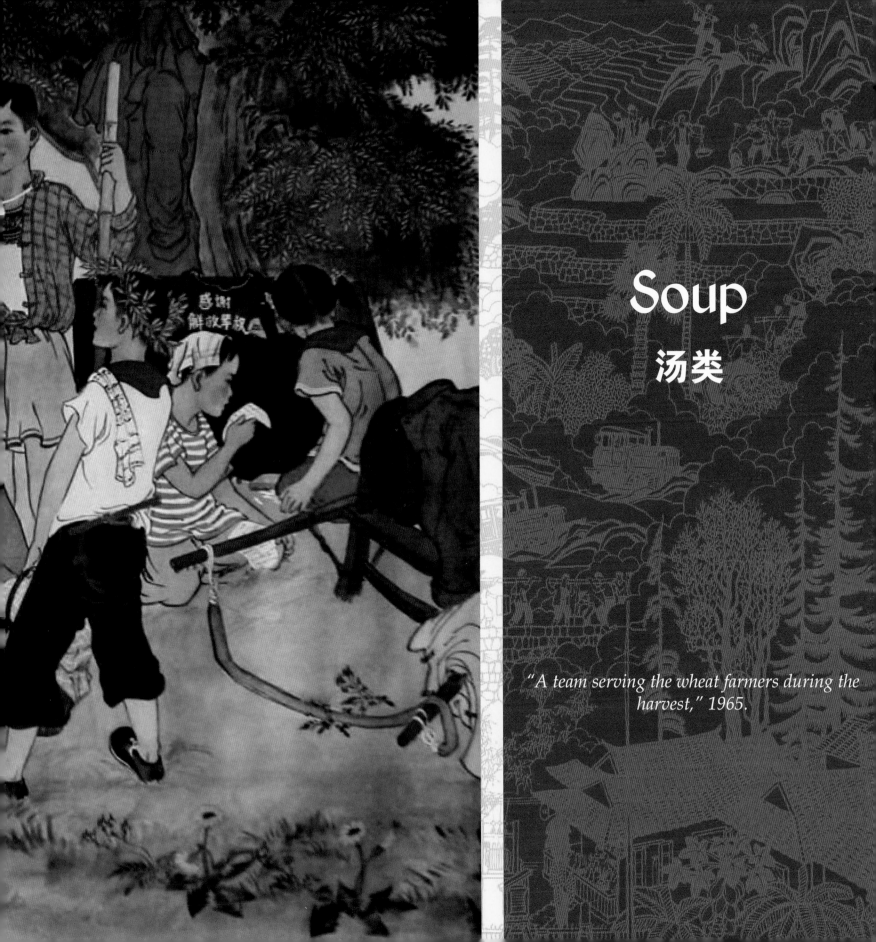

Soup

汤类

"A team serving the wheat farmers during the harvest," 1965.

三鲜炖鸡

Stewed Chicken with Three Delicacies

Ingredients

4-5 shiitake mushrooms

2.5 oz. (70 g.) bamboo shoots (half a small can)

1 whole chicken (older and tougher is better)

5-6 white mushrooms

1 piece ginger (about 1 inch, or 2.5 cm., on a side)

1 quart (about a liter) cold water

1-2 tsp. (6-12 g.) salt

Chicken is believed by some Chinese to possess mystical healing powers. It is frequently served to people who are sick or undernourished, and often stewed together with medicinal herbs like ginseng. It is usually cooked slowly to maximize its healing powers.

Scrub the mushrooms and slice the bamboo shoots into pieces about an inch (2.5 cm.) square and ¼ inch (6 mm.) thick. Then turn on the oven and set it at 250°F (120°C or gas mark ½).

Place the chicken and all the other ingredients except the salt in a large, oven-proof bowl with a cover. Cover it tightly and place it in the oven. Cook for two hours.

Remove, add salt and serve.

Chicken Stew Saves a Guerilla Fighter

One of the few so-called "revolutionary" ballets permitted to be performed in China during the Cultural Revolution was *Ode to Yimeng*. It tells the story of a poor peasant woman who came upon a wounded Communist platoon leader and resolved to nurse him back to health. He had fled to the mountains because the Nationalists had occupied his village.

The ballet portrays fighting between the Communist guerilas and the Nationalist army, and was a vehicle to demonstrate the support of the peasants for the Communists. In it, Sister Ying, living at subsistence level herself, selflessly kills and cooks a chicken, and then finds a way, at the risk of her life, to deliver the broth to the wounded officer and save him from otherwise certain death.

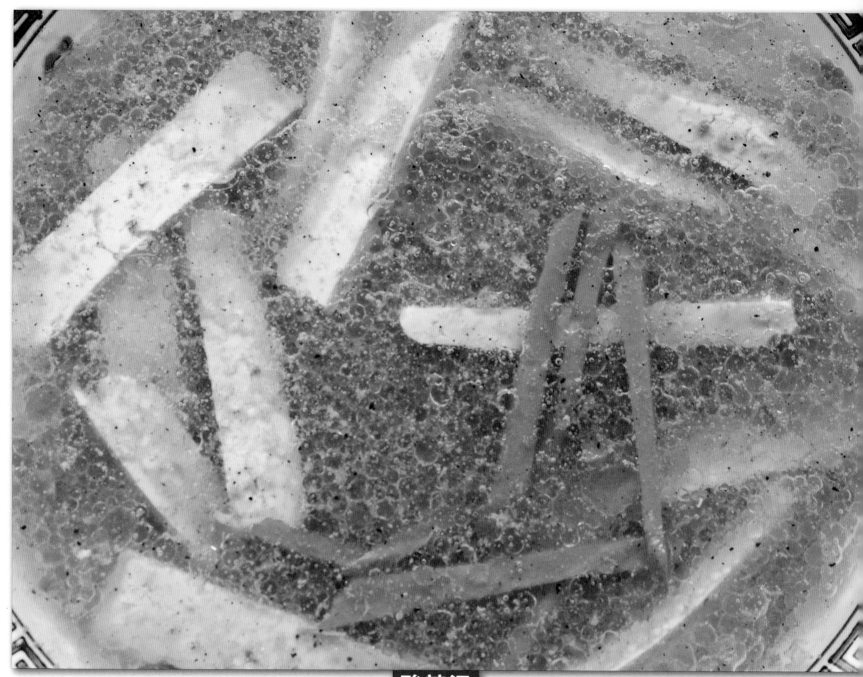

酸辣汤

Hot and Sour Soup

Ingredients

2 Tbsp. (30 g.) cornstarch
4 Tbsp. (45 ml.) cold water
½ a carrot
½ cake firm tofu
1 14.5-oz. can (or a 454 g.
   container) of chicken stock,

salted
1 egg
2 Tbsp. (30 ml.) vinegar (any
   variety except cider vinegar)
1 tsp. (2 g.) pepper
½ Tbsp. (8 ml.) sesame oil

There are references to this dish in Chinese literature as early as the Song Dynasty (960-1279 A.D.), and then as now, it was believed to possess the ability to neutralize alcohol in one's body. It is hence a traditional remedy of choice for a hangover.

Mix the cornstarch with the water to form a paste, taking care to eliminate all lumps. Slice the carrot in half lengthwise and then cut the strips into two-inch (5 cm.) lengths. Slice the tofu to match the size of the carrots.

Boil the chicken broth in a pot and add the carrots and tofu. Cook for about a minute and a half and then add the cornstarch paste. Stir it in until the soup thickens – it should do so within a few seconds. Once the soup has thickened, beat the egg in a small dish and drizzle it slowly into the soup, where it will cook quickly and form shreds in the broth. Turn off the heat and stir in the vinegar. Then add the pepper and sesame oil and serve.

Note: A vegetable broth may be substituted for the chicken stock if desired.

Cooperative Soup

Song Qingling, widow of Dr. Sun Yat-sen, the so-called "Father of Modern China," was one of a very few leaders permitted to entertain foreigners in her home during the Cultural Revolution. One dish she sometimes served was Hot and Sour Soup, which she had her cook make with bean curd and chicken blood – both gelatinous substances, one white, one red. She once explained the symbolism of this "co-operative soup" to a guest: her wish for collaboration between the Kuomintang (Nationalists) and the Communists.

蛋花玉米汤

Egg Flower and Corn Soup

Ingredients

2 Tbsp. (30 g.) cornstarch
4 Tbsp. (60 ml.) cold water
2 eggs
½ scallion (spring onion)
1 14.5-oz. can (or a 454 g. container) of chicken stock, salted

Small handful of corn kernels (frozen or canned; either is fine)
1 tsp. (5 ml.) sesame oil
Dash of pepper
2-3 sprigs of cilantro, or coriander (optional; for garnish)

Dropping beaten egg into a hot broth that has been thickened with starch creates thin shreds of egg – called "egg flowers" by the Chinese, or "egg drops" in traditional American Chinese restaurant parlance – that give dishes like this a lovely texture and appearance.

Combine the cornstarch with the water and make a paste, taking care that no lumps remain. Beat the eggs and chop the scallion on the bias into small pieces (about ¼ inch, or 6 mm., in length).

Boil the chicken stock in a pot and add the corn. When the stock boils a second time, add the cornstarch paste. It will thicken the broth in a few seconds.

Drizzle the beaten eggs into the boiling broth to create cooked shreds and then turn off the heat. Add the sesame oil, scallion and pepper. Garnish with cilantro, if desired, and serve.

Note: Vegetable broth may be substituted for the chicken broth.

Mao Buttons for an Egg

Between 1966 and 1969, China produced an estimated 2 billion buttons depicting Chairman Mao in various poses. People wore these ornaments to proclaim their loyalty to him. The largest collection of Mao badges is reportedly in the hands of Dr. Chen Xinji of Guilin, who has amassed more than 240,000. He started collecting in 1967 as an eight-year-old child in a small village. Lacking money, he traded an egg for his first few specimens.

Chen has 13,000 varieties of Mao buttons, made, variously, of steel, aluminum, porcelain, limestone, copper and even gold and silver. They show Mao in a military uniform, Mao with the Red Guards, Mao with workers, Mao against a red flag, Mao surrounded by sunflowers and many other scenes.

排骨冬菇汤

Spare Ribs and Shiitake Mushroom Soup

Ingredients

1 turnip
2 14.5-oz. cans (or two 454 g. containers) of chicken stock, salted

3-4 pork ribs
4-5 dried shiitake mushrooms

Use dried shiitake mushrooms rather than the fresh variety for this dish if they are available. They have a considerably richer flavor and keep their shape better when cooked for a long time. Tofu and other vegetables, such as celery, squash and fresh mushrooms, may be added for variety, but make sure you don't overwhelm the ribs with too much of them.

Peel and dice the turnip into cubes about an inch and a half (4 cm.) on a side. Then pour the chicken stock in a pot and add the ribs and mushrooms. Cover the pot, and place over medium heat.

Cook for 45 minutes and then add the turnip pieces. Continue cooking for an additional 15 minutes and serve.

Anything but Spare Ribs

The Cantonese love nothing so much as spare ribs, but they avoided them like the plague during the 1970s when meat was heavily rationed. The reason was simple: if you were entitled to only 250 grams of pork per month, it was the height of stupidity to accept any cut with bones in it. Far more popular, especially in the countryside, was "pork fat, four fingers thick," because it provided precious calories, oil for cooking and a wonderful taste.

Ration coupons like the one above from Pingyao, Shanxi Province, were given out by neighborhood committees and had to be used in the month indicated; if for some reason you didn't buy meat that month, you were out of luck.

汤面

Noodles in Chicken Broth

Ingredients

2 quarts (1.9 liters) of cold water

¼ lb. (115 g.) spaghetti, linguini or similar variety of noodles

1 egg

1 14.5-oz. can (or a 454 g. container) of chicken stock, salted

3-4 meatballs (made of beef, pork, chicken or turkey; optional)

½ lb. (225 g.) green vegetable (mustard greens, spinach, lettuce, cabbage or kale, for example)

This is a popular breakfast dish in China, though the optional meatballs would have been very unusual during the Cultural Revolution. In some places, when little was available other than noodles and broth, it was called "bald-headed noodles."

Bring most of the water to a boil in a pot and add the noodles. When the noodles are fully cooked, remove and drain them. Separately, boil the egg in the rest of the cold water until it is hard-boiled – about 10 minutes.

Boil the chicken broth and add the meatballs and green vegetable. Cook for 1-2 minutes. Then place the noodles in a large bowl (or in individual bowls if you wish).

Peel the egg and cut it in half, or into smaller pieces. Add the egg to the noodles. Pour in the rest of the ingredients and serve.

Soup Fit For a Prince

Mao Zedong, Peng Zhen, Prince Norodom Sihanouk and Liu Shaoqi.

For the sake of face and for propaganda purposes, the Communists always fed foreign guests very well, even when food was scarce. China saw itself as the leader of the so-called "non-aligned movement." A frequent visitor to China was Cambodia's Prince Norodom Sihanouk.

In 1973, when the Prince visited Shanghai, local officials received an order to prepare a 14-course banquet for him. Among the dishes was a chicken broth made with pre-laid eggs that required the slaughter of 108 chickens to prepare properly. Sihanouk loved it – so much so, in fact, that he reportedly ordered it again the next day!

Dessert

甜点类

"New Year's Eve in the sent-down youths' dormitory," 1977.

芒果糯米饭

Mangoes and Sticky Rice

Ingredients

1 cup (200 g.) sweet rice (also called sticky rice or glutinous rice)

3 cups (750 ml.) cold water

1 ripe mango

2-3 Tbsp. (30-45 ml.) sweetened

condensed milk (or the same amount of coconut milk mixed with 2 tsp., or 8 g., of sugar)

Yellow Asian mangoes are different from the reddish green variety available in America; they are a lot easier to peel. During the Cultural Revolution, they were seen only in China's far south, and only occasionally. If you're using the American variety, don't choose one that is overripe or it will lose its shape in this dish.

Wash and drain the rice. Soak the rice in the water in a pot for at least 10 minutes and then bring it to a boil. Turn the flame down to very low heat and simmer for approximately 5-10 more minutes, until the rice has absorbed all of the water. Remove from the flame and allow to cool.

Slice the mango in half and remove and discard the large pit. Then cut the meat of the fruit lengthwise so each piece is about a half inch (1.5 cm.) thick and the full length of the fruit, removing the peel in the process.

When the rice has cooled somewhat (but is still warm), place it on a serving plate and arrange the mango pieces around it. Then drizzle the condensed (or coconut) milk over the rice and the fruit and serve.

Mangoes for the Propaganda Teams

In 1968, Pakistan's visiting foreign minister presented Mao with a box of mangoes. The Chairman decided to share the exotic fruit with the Worker's Propaganda Team that was battling the Red Guards occupying the campus of Beijing's Tsinghua University. The gift was taken as a sign that Mao backed the workers in their struggle to restore order at the school.

A gift from Mao, who had essentially been deified by this time, was a major event. Workers lined up for a glimpse of the mangoes, which were encased in glass and which no one dared eat. Some were preserved; others were boiled in large pots of water so many people could have a sip and taste their essence. The tropical fruit became a symbol of Mao's support for the workers and peasants.

拔丝苹果

Sizzling Caramelized Apples

Ingredients

3 medium apples (any variety;
   Golden Delicious work
   especially well)
1 cup (140 g.) flour

4-5 cups (1-1.3 liters) cold water
2 cups (500 ml.) cooking oil
1½ cups (375 g.) sugar

Nobody ate this dish often during the Cultural Revolution, because sugar was too precious. It was a special treat, and could be made with potatoes, sweet potatoes or bananas as well as apples, the common denominator being a high starch content.

Core the apples; peeling them is optional. Cut each into pieces, about an inch (2.5 cm.) or an inch and a half (4 cm.) on each side. Then mix the flour with enough water to make a paste, taking care to work out all lumps. Dredge each apple piece in the flour paste, coating all sides.

Heat the oil in a wok over a high flame. When it begins to smoke, deep fry the apple pieces until they brown. Do this in stages, as there will be more pieces than the wok can handle at one time. The pieces should not touch one another while cooking. Remove the apple from the wok.

Place a bowl of cold water on the dining table. Pour most of the oil out of the wok, reserving about 2-3 tablespoons, and turn the heat down to medium. Add the sugar and stir-fry it until it dissolves. This will take a few minutes.

Return the apple pieces to the wok and stir-fry, coating each with the oil-sugar mixture. Serve immediately. Diners should plunge their apple pieces into the cold water to create long, thin threads of sugar that are very tasty.

North Korean Idylls

"Abundant apple harvest," 1965.

The few Chinese movies made during the Cultural Revolution were pure propaganda set pieces. What little diversion there was came from foreign films, but only a few were permitted, and these came exclusively from the Soviet Union, Albania and North Korea. One of the most popular was a 1971 North Korean film called "Apple Picking Time," which told tales of two sisters living under idyllic collectivism. While it, too, was blatantly propagandistic, Chinese viewers nonetheless appreciated its soothing music and colorful costumes.

芝麻糖

Sesame Seed Candy

Ingredients

1 cup (120 g.) sesame seeds   1 cup (250 g.) sugar

You may use either white or black sesame seeds to make this dish, though you might have some trouble finding the latter variety in your supermarket. Black sesame seeds, which contain more oil, give the dessert a somewhat richer flavor.

Using a flat pan, toast the sesame seeds over medium heat. They are done when you can smell their fragrance, and when a few seeds pop and begin to jump out of the pan. Remove them from the pan.

Place a wok over medium-low heat and add the sugar slowly. Stir it until it all melts into a syrup. When no more white granules are visible, add the sesame seeds and mix well.

Pour the mixture into individual molds – the bottoms of the cups in a cupcake tin are ideal if you want the candies to be round. Allow to sit for about 10 minutes until the individual pieces have solidified. Then remove and serve.

Flowering From the Bottom Up

A Cultural Revolution-era record album, "Just like the Sesame Plant, Growing So Gay."

A Chinese peasant saying about the sesame plant – that the sesame flowers from the bottom to the top – was used by the Party to send a political message during the Cultural Revolution. It signaled that the country was getting better and better, and that the changes were coming from the bottom up.

The Communists borrowed many such peasant sayings to motivate the masses, and after a time they began to wear thin. In the end, as conditions worsened, few continued to believe much, if any, of the government's constant barrage of propaganda.

153

豌豆黄

Yellow Split Pea Cake

Ingredients

¼ lb. (115 g.) yellow split peas
1 cup (250 g.) sugar (more or less, to taste)

3 cups (750 ml.) cold water
2 packages unflavored gelatin
½ cup (120 ml.) warm water

If you're used to rich European desserts, you may find this one rather basic, but it was a favorite of the Empress Dowager Cixi (1835-1908) during the late Qing Dynasty and later became a popular Beijing snack food – when split peas were available.

Place the peas, the sugar and the cold water in a pot and bring to a boil. Then turn the flame down to medium and cook until the peas become soft – about a half hour should do it.

Dissolve the gelatin in the warm water and add it to the peas. Then, using a food processor (or a food mill, which is what was used in China), puree the mixture until the peas have all disintegrated and the liquid is of a consistent texture.

Pour into a pan and allow to cool. Then cut into pieces and serve.

Note: Half a teaspoon (2-3 ml.) of vanilla extract – while not traditional – gives this dish a very pleasant flavor and can be added after the mixture is cooked. Another enhancement is to drizzle honey or a little maple syrup on top of the cake before serving.

Nixon in China

U.S. President Richard Nixon met with Mao and Premier Zhou Enlai during his historic 1972 visit to China. Nixon was fêted at a sumptuous banquet at the Great Hall of the People that included seven cold dishes (cucumbers and tomatoes; chicken in salt; vegetarian ham; deep-fried tilapia; sliced duck; preserved pork, duck and sausage; and 1,000-year eggs), six hot dishes (egg white and mushroom soup; shark's fin with bamboo shoots, chicken and ham; prawns two ways; mushrooms and green vegetables; steamed chicken with coconut; and almond cream) and seven desserts (yellow split pea cake; deep-fried spring rolls; assorted dumplings; deep-fried glutinous rice cake; bread and butter; and fried rice with ten treasures). It was on this visit that the two countries signed the Shanghai Communiqué, which committed them to work toward the normalization of diplomatic relations.

About the Authors

Sasha Gong, born and raised in China, was forced with her family from their home in Guangzhou at age nine and sent to a small village in Hunan Province. When she was permitted to return to Guangzhou, it was to a job in a candy factory. She joined the underground protest movement, and because of her "counterrevolutionary" writing, the Chinese government sent her to prison for a year. After China emerged from its madness, she earned her B.A. and M.A. degrees in history at Peking University. In 1987, she fulfilled a lifelong dream and went to the United States to study. She earned a Ph.D. in sociology from Harvard University and has held teaching posts at UCLA, George Washington University and George Mason University. Currently head of the Chinese section of the *Voice of America*, she is the author of *Born American: A Chinese Woman's Dream of Liberty* (Nimble Books, 2009). Sasha is an accomplished Chinese cook, and can whip up a feast for two or two hundred with ease.

Scott D. Seligman is a writer, historian, retired corporate executive and a career "China hand." Fluent in Mandarin and conversant in Cantonese, he lived in Taiwan, Hong Kong and China for eight years and reads and writes Chinese. He learned the art of Chinese cooking in Taiwan. He has an undergraduate degree in history from Princeton University and a master's degree in education from Harvard University. He has managed a multinational public relations agency in China and served as communications director for a Fortune 50 company. He is the author of *Chinese Business Etiquette* (Hachette, 1999) and *Dealing With the Chinese* (Warner Books, 1989) and co-author of *Chinese at a Glance* (Barron's Educational Series, 1985 and 2001) and *Now You're Talking Mandarin Chinese* (Barron's, 2006). He has also published articles in the *Asian Wall Street Journal*, the *China Business Review*, the *Jewish Daily Forward* and other publications.

Acknowledgments

The authors wish to express their appreciation to the following organizations and individuals for their assistance in this project:

For the images on pages 1, 11 (lower left), 12 (lower right), 18-19, 37, 48-49, 57, 63, 64-65, 69, 75, 77, 78-79, 81, 85, 89, 95, 108-109, 111, 120-121, 123, 129, 131, 134-135, 146-147, and 151, our heartfelt gratitude to Maopost.com and, in particular, to Pierre-Loic Lavigne, who was most generous with his time and his resources.

For the cover image, and the images on pages 43 and 90-91, our thanks to the IISH-Landsberger Collection at the International Institute of Social History in Amsterdam.

For the family photographs on pages 2, 3 and 5, our appreciation to Huang Xiuzhu and Li Pingri, Sasha Gong's aunt and uncle.

For all of the food photography throughout this book, grateful appreciation to the very talented Charles Cohan Fischl.

For ideas for improving the manuscript and shepherding it to publication, our thanks to Coleen O'Shea.

For the photograph of Scott D. Seligman that appears on page 156, our thanks to Yoma Ullman, and for the photo of the authors on page 6, our appreciation to Alice Thurston.

For help in making conversions to enable U.K. readers to follow these recipes, our gratitude to Josephine Chesterton, Anne Shepherd, Jenny Shepherd and Jenny Ullman.

For their confidence in us and in the ultimate success of this book, and their help in making it even better, thanks to Graham Earnshaw, Derek Sandhaus, Jessica Li and Frank Zheng of Earnshaw Books.